JAMESTOWN  EDUCATION

Word JOURNEYS™

ACADEMIC ENGLISH VOCABULARY

INTERMEDIATE

 McGraw Hill Glencoe

Contents

Why Use This Book?..vi

Pronunciation Guide 1

Unit 1
How Do Sports Affect Lives?..............2

Lesson 1...3

Lesson 2...11

Lesson 3...19

Unit 1 Wrap-up..27

Unit 1 Assessment...................................28

Unit 2
How Can Music Make a Difference?..30

Lesson 4...31

Lesson 5...39

Lesson 6...47

Unit 2 Wrap-up..55

Unit 2 Assessment...................................56

Unit 3
What Makes a Good Friend?...........58

Lesson 7...59

Lesson 8...67

Lesson 9...75

Unit 3 Wrap-up..83

Unit 3 Assessment...................................84

Unit 4
What Makes Me Healthy?.................. 86

Lesson 10... 87

Lesson 11... 95

Lesson 12..103

Unit 4 Wrap-up...111

Unit 4 Assessment..112

Unit 5
What Can Journeys Teach? 114

Lesson 13 115

Lesson 14..123

Lesson 15 131

Unit 5 Wrap-up...139

Unit 5 Assessment..140

Unit 6
How Does Nature Touch Lives? 142

Lesson 16..143

Lesson 17 151

Lesson 18..159

Unit 6 Wrap-up...167

Unit 6 Assessment..168

Unit 7
How Do I Measure Success?...........170

Lesson 19	171
Lesson 20	179
Lesson 21	187
Unit 7 Wrap-up	195
Unit 7 Assessment	196

Unit 8
What Makes A Great Story?...........198

Lesson 22	199
Lesson 23	207
Lesson 24	215
Unit 8 Wrap-up	223
Unit 8 Assessment	224

My Notes	226
Writing Checklist	231
Glossary	232
Image Credits	236

Why Use This Book?

This book will help you learn new words that you will use throughout your school day and beyond. You will practice reading and writing the new words.

> The **Unit Opener** asks you a question.

> Here you meet a student from another country who answers the question.

> This page also shows the Vocabulary and the Word Study topics you will find in the unit.

UNIT **1**

How Do Sports Affect Lives?

Vocabulary
attitude
contrast
devoted
element
intense
overall
positive
potential
principle
sustain

Word Study
• Compound Words with *over*
• Multiple Meanings
• Collocations

" In Brazil, I was a professional soccer player. In the United States, I play for fun. I love soccer, but I know that sports are part of my future, not all of it. "

Abdul is from Brazil.

2

Vocabulary in Context uses five of the unit vocabulary words. These words appear in blue.

Vocabulary in Context

Look at the photos and read the text. Respond to the text.

Excellent athletes are dedicated to their sport. They show that they are **devoted** to their sport by practicing on a regular schedule. Sometimes athletes participate in workouts that are very long or very difficult. These **intense** workouts help athletes improve their skills.

Describe the picture.

Practicing for a sport affects the lives of athletes. Sometimes athletes must overcome challenges to achieve their goals. Most athletes believe in an important rule. This **principle** is that returning to a sport after losing a game or being hurt is very important.

How would this principle apply to your life?

Try to find the meaning of each blue word based on its *context*, or the words around it.

Athletes want to improve. They know that winning is one part of being a good athlete. Working hard is another **element**. Some people are good at only one sport. Others do well at many different sports. You might say that these people are good **overall** athletes.

Who is your favorite athlete?

3

The **Definitions** page shows each vocabulary word with its pronunciation, part of speech, definition, and an example sentence.

In this space, you can draw your own idea of one of the words.

The **Definitions Check** allows you to check your understanding of the vocabulary words by completing three activities.

Definitions

Read the definitions and example sentences.

devoted (di-vō′-tid)
adjective loyal; dedicated
A devoted reader is a person who reads many books.

element (e′-lə-mənt)
noun a part of a whole
Fruit is one element of a healthy diet.

intense (in-tens′)
adjective extreme in strength or degree
The intense rainstorm caused damage to the tree.

overall (ō′-vər-ôl′)
adjective including everyone or everything
The overall champion won a gold medal.

principle (prin′-sə-pəl)
noun a rule or belief that forms the basis for behavior or actions
We follow the principle that every team member should help.

Choose one word to draw in this space.

4

Definitions Check

A Write the word from the box that matches the two examples in each item.

devoted	element	intense	overall	principle

1. _____
someone who volunteers many hours
a violin player who practices often

2. _____
the final grade in a class
a winner in a contest

3. _____
people should respect others
working hard is the right thing to do

4. _____
humor in a movie
one wall of a building

B Write the word from the box that relates to each group of words.

devoted	element	intense	overall	principle

_____ 1. one part, section
_____ 2. loyal, committed
_____ 3. belief, rule
_____ 4. long, extreme, hard
_____ 5. among everyone, of everything

C Write the word from the box that answers each question.

devoted	element	intense	overall	principle

1. Which word goes with *a rule for an action*? _____
2. Which word goes with *a long and difficult test*? _____
3. Which word goes with *brushing your cat every day*? _____
4. Which word goes with *a chapter in a book*? _____
5. Which word goes with *the best speller in town*? _____

5

Look on page 1 of this book for the Pronunciation Guide.

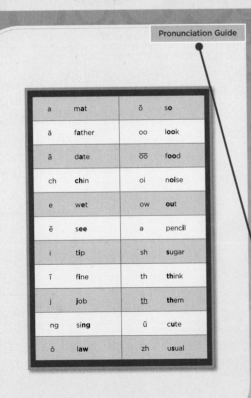

Pronunciation Guide

a	mat	ō	so
ä	father	oo	look
ā	date	o͞o	food
ch	chin	oi	noise
e	wet	ow	out
ē	see	ə	pencil
i	tip	sh	sugar
ī	fine	th	think
j	job	th	them
ng	sing	ū	cute
ô	law	zh	usual

1

In the **Reading Selection,** the five vocabulary words appear in context.

Jackie Joyner-Kersee won three gold medals.

Devoted to Sports

Jackie Joyner-Kersee was born on March 3, 1962, in East St. Louis, Illinois. As a young woman, she became interested in both basketball and in track and field. In college she became a **devoted** athlete in both sports. Joyner-Kersee was loyal to both her teams, and she practiced hard.

Practicing often and being devoted were two **elements** of her success during college. After college she focused on track and field. She participated in **intense** training, working hard to run faster and jump farther. Joyner-Kersee focused on the long jump. In this event, athletes sprint quickly to a mark and then jump as far as they can into sand.

What are other events in track and field?

Joyner-Kersee won a total of three gold medals in the Olympics of 1988 and 1992. Many people thought Joyner-Kersee was better than all of the other female track and field athletes at the Olympics. They considered her the **overall** best female athlete in track and field. Jackie Joyner-Kersee believes in being devoted to her sport. For this athlete, being devoted is an important **principle**. She follows this rule in sports and in life.

Look at the picture to predict what the reading is about. The reading is related to the question from the Unit Opener.

Comprehension Check

A Write T if the sentence is true. Write F if the sentence is false.

_____ **1.** Jackie Joyner-Kersee is an **overall** champion.

_____ **2.** There can only be one **element** of success in sports.

_____ **3.** One of Joyner-Kersee's **principles** is that being devoted to your sport is important.

_____ **4.** Joyner-Kersee never had **intense** training workouts.

_____ **5.** Joyner-Kersee was **devoted** to two sports in college.

B Write the word from the box that completes each sentence.

devoted	element	intense	overall	principle

Jackie Joyner-Kersee was a (1) _____ athlete. Being

dedicated was one (2) _____ of her success.

Working hard was another. She had (3) _____

practices. One (4) _____ Joyner-Kersee believed

in is always being devoted. She was the (5) _____

best athlete in track and field.

The **Comprehension Check** allows you to check your comprehension, or understanding, of the reading selection by completing three activities.

C Write the word from the box that replaces the underlined words.

devoted	element	intense	overall	principle

_____ **1.** Fans are <u>loyal</u> to their favorite teams.

_____ **2.** A champion displays the best ability <u>among everyone</u>.

_____ **3.** One <u>part</u> of a team effort is helping others.

_____ **4.** One basic <u>rule</u> of sports is that you should be honest when you play.

_____ **5.** Winners experience very <u>strong</u> emotions.

7

Word Study Compound Words

A compound word is made up of two or more smaller words. The compound word *overall* is made up of the smaller words *over* and *all*. Other compound words that include *over* are *overseas* and *overhead*.

Compound Word	Two Smaller Words	Meaning
overall	over and all	including everyone or everything
overseas	over and seas	abroad; across any of the oceans
overhead	over and head	above a person's head

1 *overseas* (*over* + *seas*)

Overseas is an adverb that means "across any of the oceans" and "abroad."

Some people travel <u>abroad</u> by sailing on a boat.

Some people travel overseas by sailing on a boat.

The birds migrate <u>across the ocean</u> for the winter.

The birds migrate overseas for the winter.

2 *overhead* (*over* + *head*)

Overhead is an adverb that means "above a person's head."

The dark clouds <u>above my head</u> look like rain clouds.

The dark clouds overhead look like rain clouds.

An orange fell from the tree branch <u>above our heads</u>.

An orange fell from the tree branch overhead.

There are four types of **Word Study** pages. Each lesson features one type. The title tells you what you will study:
- Multiple Meanings lessons explain different meanings of a word.
- Word Forms lessons show different forms of a word.
- Collocations lessons teach common phrases.
- Word Parts lessons tell about a word's prefix, suffix, or root.

Word Study Check Compound Words

A For each compound word, underline the first smaller word and circle the second smaller word.

Example: over(grown)

1. overall

2. overseas

3. overhead

B Circle the word that completes each sentence.

I saw rain clouds (**overhead, overall**) as I walked home. The weatherman said the rain clouds traveled (**overall, overseas**) from Asia. Then the rain poured down. Of the rainstorms we had this year, this one was the (**overall, overseas**) worst.

C Complete each sentence.

1. If I went overseas, I would visit _____
   _____

2. What I see overhead is _____
   _____

3. One of my overall best qualities is _____
   _____

D Circle the word that has a very different meaning from the other three words in its row.

1. overseas   country   vacation   neighbor

2. above   below   overhead   sky

3. element   overall   everything   total

The **Word Study Check** helps you to check your understanding of the new words or phrases you learned.

In the **Lesson Wrap-up,** you talk about what you have read with a partner by answering questions.

Then you use the ideas you talked about—and the words you have learned—to write down your thoughts.

In the **Unit Wrap-up,** you consider how well you have learned all the words in the unit.

Write your own sentences to practice using the words and prepare for the Unit Assessment.

Use the Writing Checklist on page 231 to check your writing.

Lesson 1 Wrap-up

Talk About It

Discuss questions 1–5 with a partner.

Topic:
How sports affect my life

Details:

1. Which sports are you devoted to?

2. Who is your overall favorite athlete? Why?

3. What are the most difficult elements of a sport you enjoy? Why?

4. Why should athletes have intense practices for their sports?

5. What is the most important principle for athletes to follow?

Write About It

Write about sports on the lines below. Use ideas from Talk About It.

Topic:
Sports affect my life because _____
_____

Details:

1. The sport I am most devoted to playing or watching is _____

2. My overall favorite athlete is _____

3. I think the most difficult element of my favorite sport is _____

4. Intense workouts help athletes because _____

5. The most important principle for athletes to follow is _____

10

Unit 1 Wrap-up

Think About It

Think about the words you learned in Unit 1. Have you mastered them? Write each word under the right heading: Words I Have Mastered or Words I Need to Review. Make sentences using the words to prepare for the Unit Assessment.

Vocabulary Words

attitude	overall
contrast	positive
devoted	potential
element	principle
intense	sustain

Words I Have Mastered

_____ _____
_____ _____
_____ _____
_____ _____

Words I Need to Review

_____ _____
_____ _____

Practice Sentences

_____
_____
_____
_____
_____
_____
_____
_____

Writing Checklist

1. I followed the directions for writing.
2. My writing shows that I read and understood the discussion questions.
3. I capitalized the names of people and the proper names of places and things.
4. I read aloud my writing and listened for missing words.
5. I used a dictionary to check words that didn't look right.

Use the chart below to check off the things on the list that you have done.

	✔ Writing Checklist Numbers										
Lesson Numbers	1	2	3	4	5	Lesson Numbers	1	2	3	4	5
1						13					
2						14					
3						15					
4						16					
5						17					
6						18					
7						19					
8						20					
9						21					
10						22					
11						23					
12						24					

231

Unit 1 Assessment

A Read the letters between Abdul and the Coach Selection Committee.
Circle the word that completes each sentence.

Dear Coach Selection Committee:

I would be a great coach for the nine-year-old boys' soccer league. I have
been a (**contrast, devoted**) player my whole life. I have an (**intense, attitude**)
love for the game.

In addition to my soccer skills, I also have good coaching skills. I have helped
many kids on past teams reach their (**potential, element**) on the field. My
coaching has a (**positive, principle**) effect on kids. I have the ideal (**contrast,
attitude**) for a coach.

Sincerely,
Abdul

Write a word from the box to complete each sentence.

contrast	element	overall	principle	sustain

Dear Abdul:

Thank you for your letter and positive attitude. We believe in the

(1) _____ that skills, energy, and attitude are what make a

good (2) _____ coach.

We would like to interview you. The interview is an important

(3) _____ of our hiring process. It will help us to

(4) _____ you with the other candidates. We want a

coach who can (5) _____ a team of winners all year.

Sincerely,
Al Rodriguez, Chair
Coach Selection Committee

28

B Circle the letter of the answer that best completes each sentence.

1. In contrast _____
his brother, Sam is tall.
   a. with
   b. by
   c. from

2. The prize will go to the
best _____ athlete.
   a. overhead
   b. overall
   c. overseas

3. One _____ of good
writing is a good vocabulary.
   a. element
   b. contrast
   c. attitude

4. Ira traveled _____
from New York to Madrid.
   a. overhead
   b. overall
   c. overseas

C Circle the letter of the answer that means the same thing as the
underlined words.

1. My science teacher gave us
a chart that lists all the <u>elements</u>.
   a. parts of a horse
   b. parts of chemical compounds
   c. sentences in a story

2. We saw an airplane
<u>overhead</u>.
   a. above our heads
   b. ahead of us
   c. on top of our heads

3. Bright colors are an important
<u>element</u> of the artist's style.
   a. chemical
   b. weather
   c. part

4. Keiko and Javier have always
wanted to travel <u>overseas</u>.
   a. across the country
   b. across the ocean
   c. under the sea

D For each item, write a sentence that uses both words.

1. attitude, overall

_____
_____

2. contrast, devoted

_____
_____

3. element, positive

_____
_____

29

The **Unit Assessment**
allows you to show
what you have learned
in the unit. You will
see the teenager you
met at the beginning
of the unit.

You will also complete
other activities.

My Notes

_____

_____

_____

As you work through each
lesson, write down words
you want to learn more
about in the **My Notes** pages
in the back of your book.
Later, use a dictionary to find
out more about the words,
or discuss them with your
teacher or classmates.

a	m**a**t	ō	s**o**
ä	f**a**ther	oo	l**oo**k
ā	d**a**te	o͞o	f**oo**d
ch	**ch**in	oi	n**oi**se
e	w**e**t	ow	**ou**t
ē	s**ee**	ə	penc**i**l
i	t**i**p	sh	**s**ugar
ī	f**i**ne	th	**th**ink
j	**j**ob	t̲h̲	**th**em
ng	si**ng**	ū	c**u**te
ô	l**aw**	zh	u**s**ual

How Do Sports Affect Lives?

Vocabulary
attitude
contrast
devoted
element
intense
overall
positive
potential
principle
sustain

Word Study
- Compound Words with *over*
- Multiple Meanings
- Collocations

" In Brazil, I was a professional soccer player. In the United States, I play for fun. I love soccer, but I know that sports are part of my future, not all of it. "

Abdul is from Brazil.

Vocabulary in Context

Look at the photos and read the text. Respond to the text.

Excellent athletes are dedicated to their sport. They show that they are **devoted** to their sport by practicing on a regular schedule. Sometimes athletes participate in workouts that are very long or very difficult. These **intense** workouts help athletes improve their skills.

Describe the picture.

Practicing for a sport affects the lives of athletes. Sometimes athletes must overcome challenges to achieve their goals. Most athletes believe in an important rule. This **principle** is that returning to a sport after losing a game or being hurt is very important.

How would this principle apply to your life?

Athletes want to improve. They know that winning is one part of being a good athlete. Working hard is another **element.** Some people are good at only one sport. Others do well at many different sports. You might say that these people are good **overall** athletes.

Who is your favorite athlete?

Definitions

Read the definitions and example sentences.

devoted (di-vō'-tid)

adjective loyal; dedicated

A **devoted** reader is a person who reads many books.

element (e'-lə-mənt)

noun a part of a whole

Fruit is one **element** of a healthy diet.

intense (in-tens')

adjective extreme in strength or degree

The **intense** rainstorm caused damage to the tree.

overall (ō'-vər-ôl')

adjective including everyone or everything

The **overall** champion won a gold medal.

principle (prin'-sə-pəl)

noun a rule or belief that forms the basis for behavior or actions

We follow the **principle** that every team member should help.

Choose one word to draw in this space.

Definitions Check

A Write the word from the box that matches the two examples in each item.

devoted	element	intense	overall	principle

1. _____
someone who volunteers many hours
a violin player who practices often

2. _____
the final grade in a class
a winner in a contest

3. _____
people should respect others
working hard is the right thing to do

4. _____
humor in a movie
one wall of a building

B Write the word from the box that relates to each group of words.

devoted	element	intense	overall	principle

_____ **1.** one part, section

_____ **2.** loyal, committed

_____ **3.** belief, rule

_____ **4.** long, extreme, hard

_____ **5.** among everyone, of everything

C Write the word from the box that answers each question.

devoted	element	intense	overall	principle

1. Which word goes with *a rule for an action*? _____

2. Which word goes with *a long and difficult test*? _____

3. Which word goes with *brushing your cat every day*? _____

4. Which word goes with *a chapter in a book*? _____

5. Which word goes with *the best speller in town*? _____

Jackie Joyner-Kersee won three gold medals.

Devoted to Sports

Jackie Joyner-Kersee was born on March 3, 1962, in East St. Louis, Illinois. As a young woman, she became interested in both basketball and in track and field. In college she became a **devoted** athlete in both sports. Joyner-Kersee was loyal to both her teams, and she practiced hard.

Practicing often and being devoted were two **elements** of her success during college. After college she focused on track and field. She participated in **intense** training, working hard to run faster and jump farther. Joyner-Kersee focused on the long jump. In this event, athletes sprint quickly to a mark and then jump as far as they can into sand.

What are other events in track and field?

Joyner-Kersee won a total of three gold medals in the Olympics of 1988 and 1992. Many people thought Joyner-Kersee was better than all of the other female track and field athletes at the Olympics. They considered her the **overall** best female athlete in track and field. Jackie Joyner-Kersee believes in being devoted to her sport. For this athlete, being devoted is an important **principle.** She follows this rule in sports and in life.

Comprehension Check

A Write T if the sentence is true. Write F if the sentence is false.

_____ 1. Jackie Joyner-Kersee is an **overall** champion.

_____ 2. There can only be one **element** of success in sports.

_____ 3. One of Joyner-Kersee's **principles** is that being devoted to your sport is important.

_____ 4. Joyner-Kersee never had **intense** training workouts.

_____ 5. Joyner-Kersee was **devoted** to two sports in college.

B Write the word from the box that completes each sentence.

devoted	element	intense	overall	principle

Jackie Joyner-Kersee was a (1) _____ athlete. Being

dedicated was one (2) _____ of her success.

Working hard was another. She had (3) _____

practices. One (4) _____ Joyner-Kersee believed

in is always being devoted. She was the (5) _____

best athlete in track and field.

C Write the word from the box that replaces the underlined words.

devoted	element	intense	overall	principle

_____ 1. Fans are <u>loyal</u> to their favorite teams.

_____ 2. A champion displays the best ability <u>among everyone</u>.

_____ 3. One <u>part</u> of a team effort is helping others.

_____ 4. One basic <u>rule</u> of sports is that you should be honest when you play.

_____ 5. Winners experience very <u>strong</u> emotions.

Word Study Compound Words

A compound word is made up of two or more smaller words. The compound word *overall* is made up of the smaller words *over* and *all*. Other compound words that include *over* are *overseas* and *overhead*.

Compound Word	Two Smaller Words	Meaning
overall	over and all	including everyone or everything
overseas	over and seas	abroad; across any of the oceans
overhead	over and head	above a person's head

1 *overseas (over + seas)*

Overseas is an adverb that means "across any of the oceans" and "abroad."

Some people travel <u>abroad</u> by sailing on a boat.

The birds migrate <u>across the ocean</u> for the winter.

Some people travel **overseas** by sailing on a boat.

The birds migrate **overseas** for the winter.

2 *overhead (over + head)*

Overhead is an adverb that means "above a person's head."

The dark clouds <u>above my head</u> look like rain clouds.

An orange fell from the tree branch <u>above our heads</u>.

The dark clouds **overhead** look like rain clouds.

An orange fell from the tree branch **overhead**.

Word Study Check Compound Words

A For each compound word, underline the first smaller word and circle the second smaller word.

Example: over(grown)

1. overall

2. overseas

3. overhead

B Circle the word that completes each sentence.

I saw rain clouds (**overhead, overall**) as I walked home. The weatherman said the rain clouds traveled (**overall, overseas**) from Asia. Then the rain poured down. Of the rainstorms we had this year, this one was the (**overall, overseas**) worst.

C Complete each sentence.

1. If I went overseas, I would visit _____

_____.

2. What I see overhead is _____

_____.

3. One of my overall best qualities is _____

_____.

D Circle the word that has a very different meaning from the other three words in its row.

1. overseas   country   vacation   neighbor

2. above   below   overhead   sky

3. element   overall   everything   total

Lesson 1 Wrap-up

 Talk About It

Discuss questions 1–5 with a partner.

Topic:
How sports affect my life

Details:

1. Which sports are you **devoted** to?

2. Who is your **overall** favorite athlete? Why?

3. What are the most difficult **elements** of a sport you enjoy? Why?

4. Why should athletes have **intense** practices for their sports?

5. What is the most important **principle** for athletes to follow?

 Write About It

Write about sports on the lines below. Use ideas from Talk About It.

Topic:
Sports affect my life because _____

_____.

Details:

1. The sport I am most devoted to playing or watching is _____

_____.

2. My overall favorite athlete is _____

_____.

3. I think the most difficult element of my favorite sport is

_____.

4. Intense workouts help athletes because _____

_____.

5. The most important principle for athletes to follow is _____

_____.

Vocabulary in Context

Look at the photos and read the text. Respond to the text.

Many athletes are dedicated to practicing one sport day after day to improve their skills and play well. These athletes are **devoted** to their sport. They work hard to keep their strength, speed, and skills at high levels. They want to **sustain** their abilities.

Why is it important for athletes to sustain their skills?

New athletes may have **potential,** or ability. But they must develop their potential to become successful in their sport. Many people with disabilities play sports. The disability is often just one **element,** or part, of their overall ability.

People with disabilities also work to improve their skills. Describe the picture.

Many athletes face physical challenges. Some athletes in wheelchairs play basketball. Athletes who believe in themselves and their team often do better. Their **positive** thoughts help everyone.

How do you keep a positive outlook when you want to win?

Definitions

Read the definitions and example sentences.

devoted (di-vō′-tid)

adjective loyal; dedicated

She works late because she is a **devoted** furniture builder.

element (e′-lə-mənt)

noun a part of a whole

The cake is just one **element** of a birthday party.

positive (pä′-zə-tiv)

adjective favorable; good

Holding the door for a friend is a **positive** act.

potential (pə-ten′-shəl)

noun a skill or ability that can develop

He has the **potential** to become a good guitar player.

sustain (sə-stān′)

verb to maintain or keep in existence

Water and sunlight **sustain** the plant.

Choose one word to draw in this space.

Definitions Check

A **Match the beginning of each sentence with its ending.**

_____ 1. One element of a painting   a. gave him extra help with his essay.

_____ 2. The devoted teacher   b. that I would win the game.

_____ 3. You have the potential   c. is the colors that are used.

_____ 4. To sustain good grades,   d. to become a scientist some day.

_____ 5. I had a positive feeling   e. you must study every day.

B **Put a check by the sentence that uses the bold word correctly.**

_____ 1. Our school is **devoted** to the building next door.

_____   My **devoted** sister helped me with my math homework.

_____ 2. An **element** of caring for a pet is feeding it.

_____   An aquarium is the **element** for many pet turtles.

_____ 3. We lost, but we still had **positive** things to say about the game.

_____   The game was easy to get to because it was in a **positive** location.

_____ 4. His teacher said he has the **potential** to become the mayor.

_____   The hotel has a large **potential** and many people stay there.

_____ 5. I can **sustain** three heavy books with one arm.

_____   We need to have three members in order to **sustain** the book club.

C **Circle the answer to each question. The answer is in the question. The first one has been done for you.**

1. Is a *devoted* reader (excited) or bored by books?

2. Will you probably frown or smile while thinking *positive* thoughts?

3. Which is an *element* of studying—taking notes or taking a test?

4. Should a cook with *potential* practice more or give up?

5. When you *sustain* a garden, do the plants grow or die?

Jim Abbott became an award-winning pitcher.

A Pitcher's Challenge

Jim Abbott, a talented pitcher, played professional baseball for ten years. He earned several awards throughout his career. He worked hard to **sustain** his pitching skills year after year. He also played his entire career with a disability—he has only one hand. What challenges do you think this caused for Abbott?

Abbott was born without a right hand. Yet he had the **potential** to become a great pitcher. Despite his physical challenge, Abbott was **devoted** to baseball. When he was younger, he spent many hours bouncing a ball off a wall to practice throwing and catching. Over time he developed his ability to throw a baseball with his left hand and then quickly put his baseball glove on that hand.

Abbott learned to participate fully in all **elements** of both baseball and everyday life. Despite his disability, Abbott had a **positive** attitude about himself. His good attitude and great performance resulted in many victories on and off the field. He even helped lead the 1988 U.S. Olympic baseball team to a gold medal.

Who are some other professional athletes who have overcome physical challenges?

Comprehension Check

A **Write T if the sentence is true. Write F if the sentence is false.**

_____ **1.** Jim Abbott was never a **devoted** baseball player.

_____ **2.** One **element** of Abbott's life is that he only has one hand.

_____ **3.** Abbott **sustained** his career for ten years.

_____ **4.** Abbott had the **potential** to be a great baseball player.

_____ **5.** Abbott felt **positive** about playing professional basketball.

B **Write the word from the box that completes each sentence.**

devoted	element	positive	potential	sustained

An important (1) _____ of success in sports is

practice. Even with only one hand, Jim Abbott spent many hours

(2) _____ to practicing his throwing and catching.

He knew he had the (3) _____ to play professional

baseball. He kept a (4) _____ outlook. Jim Abbott

(5) _____ a successful baseball career.

C **Write the word from the box that replaces the underlined word.**

devoted	element	positive	potential	sustained

_____ **1.** A good pitcher is one <u>part</u> of a winning baseball team.

_____ **2.** Abbott was probably <u>loyal</u> to his baseball team.

_____ **3.** Despite his disability, Abbott <u>maintained</u> a positive outlook.

_____ **4.** Practicing had a <u>good</u> impact on Abbott's playing.

_____ **5.** Abbott worked hard to develop his <u>ability</u>.

Word Study Multiple Meanings

A word often has more than one meaning. Read about two different meanings of *element*.

1 *element:* a part of a whole

- an **element** of drawing
- an **element** of cooking
- an **element** of good writing
- an **element** of safe driving

Nice shoes are one **element** of a great outfit.

> **15. Essay Question** Page 5
>
> What are your views about private schools?

The essay question was one **element** of the test.

2 *element:* in science, a basic substance; can be combined with other elements

- the **element** oxygen
- an **element** of carbon dioxide
- an **element** of water
- the symbol for the **element** helium

Oxygen is one **element** of water. The other is hydrogen.

Gold is an **element** that can be used in jewelry.

Word Study Check Multiple Meanings

A For each numbered item, choose *a* or *b* as the correct meaning of the word in bold.

element
a. a part of a whole
b. in science, a basic substance

1. _____ Trust is an **element** of friendship.

2. _____ The teacher told us about copper, which is an **element**.

3. _____ Scientists study the chemical **elements**.

4. _____ Exercise is an **element** of good health.

B Write "Yes" or "No" to answer each question.

_____ 1. Can you practice the elements of iodine?

_____ 2. Can you learn the elements of reading?

_____ 3. Is a book an element of a chapter?

_____ 4. Is a keyboard an element of a computer system?

_____ 5. Is there a symbol for the element gold?

_____ 6. Can you combine two or more elements?

C Follow the directions below. Write your answers on the lines.

1. List two **elements** of a normal school day.

_____

_____

2. List two chemical **elements**.

_____

_____

Lesson 2 Wrap-up

 Talk About It

Discuss questions 1–5 with a partner.

Topic:
How sports can be challenging

Details:

1. What sport are you most devoted to playing or watching?

2. What element of that sport is most challenging?

3. How do athletes sustain their ability to play that sport?

4. Why is it important to be positive when facing challenges?

5. How do young athletes in this sport develop their potential?

 Write About It

Write about challenges in sports on the lines below. Use ideas from Talk About It.

Topic:
Sports can be challenging because _____

_____.

Details:

1. The sport I am most devoted to is _____

2. The most challenging element of this sport is _____

_____.

3. Athletes sustain their playing skills by _____

_____.

4. Being positive when facing challenges is important because

_____

_____.

5. Young athletes in this sport develop their potential by

_____

_____.

Vocabulary in Context

Look at the photos and read the text. Respond to the text.

Learning a new sport can help you use your skills. Many people have the ability to play a sport well. They just need to develop this **potential**.

Having talent is important. But most athletes believe in the **principle** that practice is just as important. To be better players, they follow this belief. Describe the picture.

Many people who learn a new sport develop more confidence in their physical abilities. They develop a good **attitude** about what they are capable of doing. Learning a new sport can have other **positive** effects too. Athletes may feel stronger and healthier than people who do not play a sport.

How else can sports help you?

How can you choose a new sport? You might look at how sports are different. You can **contrast** them by looking at which skills they require. For example, basketball, tennis, and soccer all require different skills.

What sport best matches your skills?

Definitions

Read the definitions and example sentences.

attitude (a'-tə-tōōd')

noun a mental state or feeling

Celia has a bad **attitude** about working on group projects.

contrast (kən-trast')

verb to find differences between two or more people or things

He will **contrast** the colors in the two paintings.

positive (pä'-zə-tiv)

adjective favorable; good

I got a **positive** response from everyone who ate my cake.

potential (pə-ten'-shəl)

noun a skill or ability that can develop

She has the **potential** to become a great singer.

principle (prin'-sə-pəl)

noun a rule or belief that forms the basis for behavior or actions

Mrs. Torres believes in the **principle** that people should be on time.

Choose one word to draw in this space.

Definitions Check

A **Put a check by the answer to each question.**

1. Which sentence is an example of someone with a good attitude?
   _____ My brother will practice harder after he loses a game.
   _____ My sister quit the soccer team after they lost a game.

2. Which sentence is an example of how you can contrast two animals?
   _____ The zebra is short, but the giraffe is tall.
   _____ The zebra is standing next to the giraffe.

3. Which sentence is an example of people doing something positive?
   _____ After school, my friends and I pick up litter in the park.
   _____ After school, my friends and I see a lot of litter in the park.

4. Which sentence is an example of students developing their potential?
   _____ During class, I talk with my friends about the weekend.
   _____ Before a test, our study group meets to review our questions.

B **Write the word from the box that completes each sentence.**

attitude	contrast	positive	potential	principle

1. One _____ is that being honest is important.

2. Helping with chores is a _____ thing to do.

3. I can develop my _____ by practicing.

4. Tourists compare and _____ cities they visit.

5. People like him because of his cheerful _____.

C **Complete the sentences below.**

1. My attitude is usually _____.

2. Two things I contrast are _____.

3. One positive thing I do is _____.

4. I have the potential to _____.

5. I believe in the principle of _____.

Teens practice as a group.

Trying New Sports and Making New Friends

If you **contrast** skateboarding and snowboarding, you will uncover many differences between the sports. A skateboarder uses a board with wheels and practices on sidewalks and ramps. A snowboarder also uses a board, but it has no wheels and it can only glide on snowy hills. How can you contrast skateboarding and snowboarding with in-line skating?

Many skateboarders and snowboarders feel good about their sports and about the people who participate in them. They have good **attitudes.** This makes it easier for them to make new friends with other skateboarders or snowboarders. Some join skateboarding and snowboarding groups. Practicing with a group of people can be **positive** for those who do it. They have fun and learn from one another.

These two sports are similar in one way. People can enjoy them as a group. People who practice in a group have the **potential** to improve more than those who practice alone. They have more help developing or improving their skills. Working together and helping each other are two **principles** that many athletes believe in. They are basic rules that many athletes follow when they practice in a group.

What are other rules for practicing in a group?

Comprehension Check

A **Write T if the sentence is true. Write F if the sentence is false.**

_____ 1. Practicing stops you from developing your **potential**.

_____ 2. Having a good **attitude** may help people make friends.

_____ 3. Skateboarding in a group can be **positive**.

_____ 4. There is no way to **contrast** skateboarding and snowboarding.

_____ 5. A **principle** of practicing in a group is that everyone should help one another.

B **Write the word from the box that completes each sentence.**

attitude	contrast	positive	potential	principle

You can develop your (1) _____ if you practice sports in a group. You can (2) _____ other people's skill with your own. One (3) _____ of practicing in a group is to work together. It is important to have a good (4) _____. Making new friends can be a (5) _____ part of being in a group.

C **Write the word from the box that replaces the underlined words.**

attitude	contrast	positive	potential	principle

_____ 1. You can have a good or bad <u>mental state</u>.

_____ 2. You can develop your <u>skill or ability</u> by watching others.

_____ 3. The same <u>rules</u> apply to many different sports.

_____ 4. Your experience will be <u>good</u> if you work with friends.

_____ 5. Some people <u>compare the differences between</u> skateboarding and snowboarding.

Word Study Collocations

A collocation is a phrase or group of words that people use a lot. There are two collocations that use the word *contrast.* They have the same meaning.

1 *in contrast to:* as compared to something else
- The flower garden smells nice in contrast to the nearby landfill.
- The skyscraper is tall in contrast to other nearby buildings.

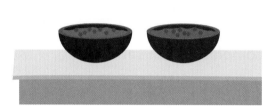

The red salsa is mild in contrast to the spicy green salsa.

Olga looks happy in contrast to her brother.

2 *in contrast with:* as compared with something else
- The flower garden smells nice in contrast with the nearby landfill.
- The skyscraper is tall in contrast with other nearby buildings.

Tomas got many gifts this year in contrast with last year.

Edward is tall in contrast with his sister.

Word Study Check Collocations

A Rewrite each sentence on the line below it. Replace the underlined words with the collocation in parentheses.

1. (in contrast with)
   He looks sad <u>as compared with</u> his friend.

   _____

2. (in contrast to)
   The car is small <u>as compared to</u> the truck.

   _____

3. (in contrast to)
   The farmer grew a lot of corn <u>as compared to</u> last year.

   _____

B Circle the word that does not belong with the others in its row. The first one is done for you.

1. talk about athletes in contrast to:

   musicians   (flowers)   teachers   mechanics

2. discuss movies in contrast with:

   books   plays   musicals   cameras

3. write about fruit in contrast to:

   meat   vegetables   plates   bread

C Complete the sentences below.

1. It is better to arrive on time in contrast to _____.

2. People may talk about football in contrast to _____.

3. I am tall in contrast with _____.

4. I am short in contrast with _____.

5. Grapes taste sweet in contrast with _____.

Lesson 3 Wrap-up

 Talk About It

Discuss questions 1–5 with a partner.

Topic:
How learning a new sport might affect my life

Details:

1. Why is it important to have a good **attitude** when learning a new sport?

2. What is **positive** about practicing a sport in a group?

3. How can an athlete develop his or her **potential** in a new sport?

4. Why might someone want to **contrast** one sport with another?

5. What **principle** would you follow when learning a new sport?

 Write About It

Write about learning new sports on the lines below. Use ideas from Talk About It.

Topic:
Learning a new sport might affect my life because _____

_____.

Details:

1. When learning a new sport, having a good attitude will _____

_____.

2. Practicing with a group is positive because _____

_____.

3. An athlete can develop his or her potential by _____

_____.

4. A person may contrast two sports in order to _____

_____.

5. One principle to follow when learning a new sport is

_____.

Unit 1 Wrap-up

 ## Think About It

Think about the words you learned in Unit 1. Have you mastered them? Write each word under the right heading: Words I Have Mastered or Words I Need to Review. Make sentences using the words to prepare for the Unit Assessment.

Vocabulary Words

attitude	overall
contrast	positive
devoted	potential
element	principle
intense	sustain

Words I Have Mastered

_____   _____

_____   _____

_____   _____

_____   _____

Words I Need to Review

_____   _____

_____   _____

_____   _____

Practice Sentences

_____

_____

_____

_____

_____

_____

_____

_____

Unit 1 Assessment

A Read the letters between Abdul and the Coach Selection Committee. Circle the word that completes each sentence.

Dear Coach Selection Committee:

I would be a great coach for the nine-year-old boys' soccer league. I have been a (**contrast, devoted**) player my whole life. I have an (**intense, attitude**) love for the game.

In addition to my soccer skills, I also have good coaching skills. I have helped many kids on past teams reach their (**potential, element**) on the field. My coaching has a (**positive, principle**) effect on kids. I have the ideal (**contrast, attitude**) for a coach.

Sincerely,
Abdul

Write a word from the box to complete each sentence.

contrast	element	overall	principle	sustain

Dear Abdul:

Thank you for your letter and positive attitude. We believe in the

(1) _____ that skills, energy, and attitude are what make a

good (2) _____ coach.

We would like to interview you. The interview is an important

(3) _____ of our hiring process. It will help us to

(4) _____ you with the other candidates. We want a

coach who can (5) _____ a team of winners all year.

Sincerely,
Al Rodriguez, Chair
Coach Selection Committee

B Circle the letter of the answer that best completes each sentence.

1. In contrast _____
his brother, Sam is tall.
  a. with
  b. by
  c. from

2. The prize will go to the
best _____ athlete.
  a. overhead
  b. overall
  c. overseas

3. One _____ of good
writing is a good vocabulary.
  a. element
  b. contrast
  c. attitude

4. Ira traveled _____
from New York to Madrid.
  a. overhead
  b. overall
  c. overseas

C Circle the letter of the answer that means the same thing as the underlined words.

1. My science teacher gave us
a chart that lists all the <u>elements</u>.
  a. parts of a horse
  b. parts of chemical compounds
  c. sentences in a story

2. We saw an airplane
<u>overhead</u>.
  a. above our heads
  b. ahead of us
  c. on top of our heads

3. Bright colors are an important
<u>element</u> of the artist's style.
  a. chemical
  b. weather
  c. part

4. Keiko and Javier have always
wanted to travel <u>overseas</u>.
  a. across the country
  b. across the ocean
  c. under the sea

D For each item, write a sentence that uses both words.

1. attitude, overall

_____

_____

2. contrast, devoted

_____

_____

3. element, positive

_____

_____

How Can Music Make a Difference?

Vocabulary
appropriate
aspect
diverse
enhance
evolve
expand
flexible
incorporate
transform
unique

Word Study
- Word Forms
- The Prefix *in-*
- Multiple Meanings

"When I get sad or angry, I listen to music to get relaxed and happy again. It helps me through all the rough times."

Weiyin's family is from China.

Vocabulary in Context

Look at the photos and read the text. Respond to the text.

The world is home to a variety of people. The people are **diverse.** The music and dance they enjoy are also diverse. Many cultures have their own traditional dances that are unlike other kinds of dances. These dances are **unique** to each culture.

What traditional dances do you know about?

The cherry blossom dance in Japan is an example of a traditional dance. Dances can change or develop slowly over a long period of time, sometimes hundreds of years. They **evolve.**

How might a dance evolve?

Sometimes people change a traditional dance for a reason. One part of a dance people might **transform** is the number of people who participate. A large celebration might include many performers. Another **aspect** of a dance that might change is the clothes dancers wear. The clothes' colors or patterns may evolve over time.

What traditional dances have you seen?

Definitions

Read the definitions and example sentences.

aspect (as'-pekt')

noun a particular part, feature, or characteristic of something

One **aspect** of the computer is its large screen.

diverse (dī-vərs')

adjective made up of various qualities or kinds

My **diverse** group of friends includes people from all over the world.

evolve (i-välv')

verb to develop over time or in stages

An artist's skills may **evolve** and improve over time.

transform (trans-fôrm')

verb to change in nature or condition

The ice cube will **transform** into a puddle in the sun.

unique (yoo-nēk')

adjective being the only one of its type

The natural pattern of each snowflake is **unique.**

Choose one word to draw in this space.

Definitions Check

A Write the word from the box that matches the two examples in each item.

aspect	diverse	evolve	transform	unique

1. _____
a snowflake
a person's fingerprints

2. _____
to become a better English speaker
to become wiser over time

3. _____
thirty different flavors of ice cream
people from six different countries

4. _____
the size of a jacket
the color of a mug

B Write the word from the box that relates to each group of words.

aspect	diverse	evolve	transform	unique

_____ 1. develop, progress

_____ 2. feature, part, characteristic

_____ 3. special, only, different

_____ 4. various, different, assorted

_____ 5. make over, change

C Write the word from the box that answers each question.

aspect	diverse	evolve	transform	unique

1. Which word goes with *to grow and change slowly*? _____

2. Which word goes with *different from all others*? _____

3. Which word goes with *to change a thing*? _____

4. Which word goes with *variety in a group of kids*? _____

5. Which word goes with *one part of how you look*? _____

Participants dance for charity.

A Dance to Raise Dollars

Dance marathons became popular in the 1920s. During these contests, people danced for long periods of time, even as long as a month. They danced to win money or even for the free food. How would you feel after dancing for a month?

Beginning in the 1970s, dance marathons **transformed** into something very different. People no longer danced for free food. One **aspect** of dance marathons today is that they raise money for others. People donate money for each hour that someone dances. The longer the marathons last, the more money is raised.

Dance marathons at universities help **diverse** groups. A marathon might raise money for an animal shelter, a food pantry, or another charity. These dance marathons often continue for 48 hours, and dancers have fun while helping others.

In 1973 a dance marathon at Pennsylvania State University raised $2,000 for charity. The event was not **unique** because the university started to hold marathons every year. The plans for this event have **evolved** since that first marathon in 1973. The small dance marathon has developed into a very large event. In 2007 the Pennsylvania State dance raised more than $5 million!

Would you dance for a charity? Which one?

Comprehension Check

A Write T if the sentence is true. Write F if the sentence is false.

_____ 1. Dance marathons **transformed** into events for charities.

_____ 2. The Pennsylvania State dance marathon in 1973 was a **unique** event.

_____ 3. The Pennsylvania State dance marathon has **evolved** since 1973.

_____ 4. Dance marathons raise money for **diverse** causes.

_____ 5. A new **aspect** of dance marathons is that they are long.

B Write the word from the box that completes each sentence.

aspect	diverse	evolved	transformed	unique

In the 1970s, people (1) _____ dance

marathons into something new. The dance marathon in 1973 was not a

(2) _____ event. It (3) _____

over time and raised $5 million in 2007. One (4) _____

of dance marathons is that they raise money for good causes. The money

goes to (5) _____ charities.

C Write the word from the box that replaces the underlined words.

aspect	diverse	evolved	transformed	unique

_____ 1. Dance marathons raise money for <u>many different</u> causes.

_____ 2. Dance marathons have <u>changed over time</u>.

_____ 3. The purpose of dance marathons <u>changed greatly</u>.

_____ 4. One <u>feature</u> of dance marathons is their length.

_____ 5. The Pennsylvania State dance marathon was not <u>one of a kind</u>.

Word Study Word Forms

Words often have several different forms. Read below about some of the different word forms of *transform.*

1 *transformer* (noun)

A *transformer* is a device that changes electricity into a current of higher or lower voltage.

A microphone uses a device to **transform** a small electrical signal into a bigger one.

A microphone uses a **transformer**.

The phone charger has a part that **transforms** the electrical current.

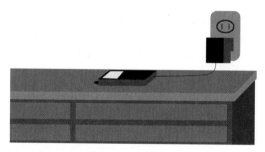

The phone charger has a **transformer**.

2 *transformation* (noun)

A change in nature or condition is a *transformation.*

Alan wears a fake nose to **transform** into his character.

Alan's **transformation** into his character includes wearing a fake nose.

The heavy storm **transformed** the landscape.

The heavy storm caused a **transformation** in the landscape.

Word Study Check Word Forms

A **Circle the word that completes each sentence.**

A (**transform, transformer**) changes electricity. This device can

(**transformation, transform**) a small electrical signal into a bigger one.

The device makes these (**transformations, transforming**) so you can use

electricity more easily.

B **Complete each sentence.**

1. One transformation that happens in nature is _____

    _____ .

2. My life was transformed when _____

    _____ .

3. One place I have seen a transformer is _____

    _____ .

C **Match each word to its meaning.**

_____ 1. transform   **a.** a device that changes electricity

_____ 2. transformation   **b.** to change in nature or condition

_____ 3. transformer   **c.** a change in nature or condition

D **Write the word from the box that completes each sentence.**

transform	transformers	transformation

1. Power lines have _____ so homes can use
    electricity.

2. Education will _____ your life.

3. Neighbors were amazed at the house's _____ .

37

Lesson 4 Wrap-up

Talk About It

Discuss questions 1–5 with a partner.

Topic:
How music and dance affect people's lives

Details:

1. How can music and dance be **diverse**?

2. How do music and dance **evolve** over time?

3. How can music and dance **transform** people?

4. What **aspects** of dance do you like the most? The least?

5. What is your favorite dance? Why is it **unique**?

Write About It

Write about music and dance on the lines below. Use ideas from Talk About It.

Topic:
Music and dance affect people's lives because _____

_____.

Details:

1. Music and dance can be diverse because _____

_____.

2. Music and dance evolve over time through _____

_____.

3. Music and dance can transform people by _____

_____.

4. One aspect of dance I like best is _____.

One aspect I like least is _____.

5. My favorite dance is _____.

It is unique because _____

_____.

Vocabulary in Context

Look at the photos and read the text. Respond to the text.

Music is powerful and can bring people together. Music has a **unique** effect on people. Listening to music affects people differently than seeing a painting or reading a poem does.

Music may **transform** the way people feel. It can make people happy when they are sad and wake them up when they are tired. How does music transform the way you feel?

The sounds of music can come from unexpected places, and almost anything can become an instrument. For example, because a saw is **flexible,** you can bend it. Then you can create musical sounds by moving a bow across it.

What unusual instruments have you seen?

You can create music with one instrument, or you can **incorporate** several other instruments. By adding drums and a special beat, you can improve the rhythm of the sound. You can also **enhance** the sound by adding vocals.

What else can enhance music?

Definitions

Read the definitions and example sentences.

enhance (in-hans′)

verb to make greater in beauty, quality, or value; to add to

A new haircut will **enhance** the dog's appearance.

flexible (flek′-sə-bəl)

adjective easy to bend without breaking

The garden hose can bend around the corner because it is **flexible.**

incorporate (in-kôr′-pə-rāt′)

verb to combine a part or parts into a larger whole

I will **incorporate** another color into my painting.

transform (trans-fôrm′)

verb to change in nature or condition

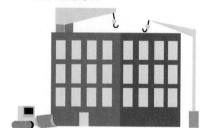

They will **transform** the old hotel into a hospital.

unique (yoo-nēk′)

adjective being the only one of its type

The sculpture is **unique** because there is not another one like it.

Choose one word to draw in this space.

Definitions Check

A Match the beginning of each sentence with its ending.

_____ 1. I will enhance the food by

_____ 2. A belt should be flexible,

_____ 3. I will incorporate

_____ 4. The magician will transform

_____ 5. A unique idea is

a. some jokes into my speech.

b. adding spices.

c. unlike any other one.

d. the scarves into a flower.

e. not stiff.

B Put a check by the sentence that uses the bold word correctly.

_____ 1. The dancer could bend her **flexible** legs very easily.

_____ The dancer could not stand up on her **flexible** legs.

_____ 2. I will **enhance** my story by adding details.

_____ I will **enhance** a mustache before winter.

_____ 3. I will **incorporate** into a doctor when I grow up.

_____ I will **incorporate** pictures into my report.

_____ 4. We will **transform** the books onto new bookshelves.

_____ A book can **transform** the way you think about something.

_____ 5. Each snowflake is **unique**.

_____ Green grass is **unique**.

C Circle the answer to each question. The answer is in the question. The first one has been done for you.

1. Do you _enhance_ a car by (washing it) or crashing it?

2. Is it easy or difficult to bend something _flexible_?

3. When you _incorporate_ something, do you add it or take it away?

4. To _transform_ something, do you ignore it or change it?

5. Is something _unique_ if you have only one or many?

Group members play a large marimba.

Music Connects to Culture

The marimba is Guatemala's national instrument. A marimba is a wooden keyboard instrument. The people of Guatemala **incorporate** marimba music into many parts of their lives. The marimba is also popular in other Central American countries, in Africa, and in South America.

In the 1980s, many people from Guatemala moved to the United States to escape a war. The change **transformed** their lives. They had to learn a new language and a new way of life. Some of them were parents who wanted their children to keep traditions from Guatemala. They helped their children form Marimba Oxib K'ajau, a marimba group.

Today, the Oxib K'ajau group performs all over the United States. They play a **unique** marimba. It is large enough that several players can play it at once. The players need to be **flexible** to reach across the huge keyboard. What would it be like to play the marimba?

The young members must practice hard to learn to play the large marimba. In return, they learn about Guatemalan culture and teach others what they learn. Being in the group **enhances** their lives and connects them to people of other cultures. How can music enhance your life?

Comprehension Check

A Write T if the sentence is true. Write F if the sentence is false.

_____ 1. Music cannot **enhance** someone's life.

_____ 2. Many Guatemalans **incorporate** marimba music into their lives.

_____ 3. A war **transformed** the lives of many Guatemalans.

_____ 4. Oxib K'ajau plays a marimba that is **unique.**

_____ 5. A large marimba is more **flexible** than a small marimba.

B Write the word from the box that completes each sentence.

enhances	flexible	incorporate	transformed	unique

Music (1) _____ our lives. When people

from Guatemala moved to the United States, their lives were

(2) _____. Some of them formed a group to

play a (3) _____ marimba. Players must be

(4) _____ to reach across the large instrument.

Many Guatemalans (5) _____ marimba music

into their lives.

C Write the word from the box that replaces the underlined words.

enhances	flexible	incorporate	transformed	unique

_____ 1. The people in Oxib K'ajau are <u>able to bend their bodies</u>, so they can reach across the marimba.

_____ 2. Music <u>improves</u> the lives of many people.

_____ 3. A war <u>changed</u> the lives of many Guatemalans.

_____ 4. The marimba used by Oxib K'ajau is <u>one of a kind</u>.

_____ 5. Guatemalans <u>include</u> marimba music in their lives.

Word Study The Prefix *in-*

A prefix is a part of a word that has a meaning of its own. It comes at the beginning of a word. A common prefix is *in-*. Some words that have this prefix are *incorporate, insight,* and *indoors.*

Word	Prefix	Root	Meaning
incorporate	*in* = in, into, or within	from the Latin word *corpus* = body	to combine a part or parts into a larger body or whole
insight		*sight* = the power of seeing	the power of seeing into or understanding something
indoors		*door* = the part of a building for entering or leaving	in or into a building

1 *insight* (*in* + *sight*)

The word *sight* means "the power of seeing." **Insight** is a noun that means "the power of seeing into or understanding something."

We use our <u>power of seeing</u> into history to learn lessons from it.

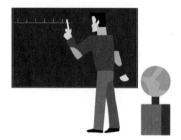

We use our **insight** into history to learn lessons from it.

Doctors have great <u>understanding</u> when it comes to the body.

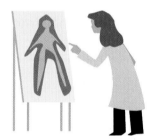

Doctors have great **insight** when it comes to the body.

2 *indoors* (*in* + *door* + *s*)

The word *door* means "the part of a building for entering or leaving." **Indoors** is an adverb that means "in or into a building."

When it began raining, we ran <u>into the house</u>.

When it began raining, we ran **indoors**.

We must stay <u>inside the school</u> until we finish our work.

We must stay **indoors** until we finish our work.

Word Study Check The Prefix *in-*

A For each word, circle the prefix and underline the rest of the word.

Example: (in)come

1. incorporate

2. insight

3. indoors

B Circle the word that completes each sentence.

Before school, I ran through the (**indoors, doors**) just before the bell rang.

During history class, I gained (**insight, sight**) into the causes of the Civil

War. I took notes during many classes. After school, I plan to (**corporate,**

incorporate) the notes into a list called "Important Things I've Learned."

C Complete each sentence.

1. When I'm indoors at home, I like to _____

_____.

2. One thing I have insight into is _____

_____.

3. I usually incorporate _____

_____ into my schedule every day.

D Circle the word that has a very different meaning from the other three words in its row.

1. incorporate   combine   mix   ignore

2. within   weather   indoors   inside

3. understanding   sleeping   seeing   insight

Lesson 5 Wrap-up

 Talk About It

Discuss questions 1–5 with a partner.

Topic:
Learning about cultures through music

Details:

1. How is music **incorporated** into cultures you know about?

2. How can music **enhance** your insight into a different culture?

3. How can being **flexible** help a person play an instrument?

4. What is **unique** about your culture's music?

5. How has music **transformed** you or someone you know?

Write About It

Write about music and culture on the lines below. Use ideas from Talk About It.

Topic:
I learn about different cultures through music by _____

_____.

Details:

1. Music can be incorporated into a culture by _____

_____.

2. Music enhances my understanding of a different culture because

_____

_____.

3. Being flexible can help a person play an instrument because

_____.

4. One unique thing about my culture's music is _____

_____.

5. I think that music can transform someone's life because

_____.

Vocabulary in Context

Look at the photos and read the text. Respond to the text.

The technology of recorded music has changed over the years. Early records were made of vinyl. These records were **appropriate** for listening to music at home, but not away from home. The record player was too large to carry. What kind of music might you hear on a vinyl record?

Compact discs, or CDs, became popular in the 1990s. CD players are smaller than record players. Another **aspect** of CD technology is the improved sound quality. Many people think that CDs can **enhance** the quality of the music. Do you have any CDs? What are some of the titles?

After CDs came MP3 players. An MP3 player holds many songs in the form of computer files. MP3 players have allowed people to **expand** the collection of music they carry with them. They can keep many different kinds of music together. Are your favorite songs **diverse,** or all the same style? Explain.

Definitions

Read the definitions and example sentences.

appropriate (ə-prō′-prē-ət)

adjective fitting or suitable

Gabriela's dress was **appropriate** for the fancy restaurant.

aspect (as′-pekt′)

noun a particular part, feature, or characteristic of something

A good diet is one **aspect** of a healthy life.

diverse (dī-vərs′)

adjective made up of various qualities or kinds

Desmond's dogs are **diverse.**

enhance (in-hans′)

verb to make greater; to add to

Spices **enhance** the flavor of food.

expand (ik-spand′)

verb to make or grow larger

If you blow into a balloon, it will **expand.**

Choose one word to draw in this space.

Definitions Check

A Put a check by the answer to each question.

1. Which sentence is an example of appropriate behavior?
   _____ I played loud music in the library.
   _____ I read quietly in the library.

2. Which sentence is an example of something that is diverse?
   _____ My soccer team is for girls only.
   _____ The museum's collection has many styles of art.

3. Which sentence shows how one thing can enhance another thing?
   _____ I got a red sweater and bicycle for my birthday.
   _____ That red sweater makes Elena's skirt look prettier.

4. Which sentence is an example of making something expand?
   _____ I filled the tire with air.
   _____ I filled the metal can with trash.

B Write the word from the box that completes each sentence.

appropriate	aspect	diverse	enhance	expand

1. A rubber band will _____ if you pull it.

2. It is not _____ to eat with your mouth open.

3. My friends have _____ interests.

4. Salt will _____ the flavor of the soup.

5. I studied every _____ of the problem.

C Complete the sentences below.

1. The population of the United States is diverse because _____
   _____.

2. An important aspect of being a student is _____.

3. I can expand my knowledge of geography by _____.

4. I can enhance my health by _____.

5. During a class, it is not appropriate to _____.

These teenagers are enjoying music at a party.

Why Is Music Important to Teens?

Many teenagers in the United States listen to music for hours each day. Music can influence many **aspects** of teens' lives. It can have an impact on how they speak, what they wear, and who their friends are. Teens sometimes use music to **enhance** their moods. For example, if you are feeling sad, the right song can make you feel better. Why is music important to you?

Teens may be in the same age group, but their taste in music is **diverse.** They enjoy many different music styles, including pop, hip-hop, jazz, country, and rock. Adults do not always agree about what is **appropriate** for teens to hear. Some adults think that certain songs are bad for teens. As a result, some CDs now have warning stickers. In your opinion, what makes a song appropriate for teens?

Many teens make music as well as listen to it. They play in school orchestras, sing in choirs, or form rock bands with their friends. These activities **expand** and strengthen teenagers' interest in music. For example, a teen who plays in a school orchestra could develop an interest in classical music. How does music affect your life?

Comprehension Check

A **Write T if the sentence is true. Write F if the sentence is false.**

_____ 1. One **aspect** of music is the mood it creates.

_____ 2. **Diverse** types of music are available to teens.

_____ 3. Music cannot **enhance** a person's mood.

_____ 4. Most adults think that all music is **appropriate** for teens.

_____ 5. School activities can **expand** a teen's interest in music.

B **Write the word from the box that completes each sentence.**

appropriate	aspects	diverse	enhance	expanding

Teens listen to (1) _____ styles of music. This music

can influence many (2) _____ of teens' lives. Some

music can even (3) _____ a teen's mood. The

amount of music for sale is (4) _____ all the time.

But many adults do not think that all music is (5) _____

for teens.

C **Write the word from the box that replaces the underlined words.**

appropriate	aspect	diverse	enhance	expand

_____ 1. Some adults think certain music is not <u>suitable</u> for young people to listen to.

_____ 2. Playing an instrument can <u>broaden</u> a teen's interest in music.

_____ 3. An important <u>feature</u> of music is how it makes us feel.

_____ 4. Happy music can <u>improve</u> a person's mood.

_____ 5. Teens have <u>different</u> interests.

Word Study   Multiple Meanings

The same word often has more than one meaning. Read about two different meanings of *appropriate.*

1 *appropriate:*   (adjective) fitting or suitable
- appropriate clothes for the weather
- appropriate gift for her birthday
- appropriate behavior
- appropriate tools for a job

I wear appropriate clothes when it is cold outside.

I used the appropriate tools to hang the picture on the wall.

2 *appropriate:*   (verb) to take for yourself; to use as your own
- appropriate government money
- appropriate someone's identity
- appropriate a homeland
- appropriate a house

The government passed a bill to appropriate money for education.

People from Europe appropriated the homelands of many native peoples.

Word Study Check Multiple Meanings

A For each numbered item, choose *a* or *b* as the correct meaning of the word in bold.

appropriate
a. (adjective) fitting or suitable
b. (verb) to take for yourself; to use as your own

1. _____ The bank **appropriated** her property.

2. _____ It is **appropriate** to raise your hand in class before speaking.

3. _____ It is **appropriate** to be polite around adults.

4. _____ The enemy army **appropriated** the church as a base.

B Write "Yes" or "No" to answer each question.

_____ **1.** Is it appropriate to copy another student's homework?

_____ **2.** Is it appropriate to wear nice clothes to a nice restaurant?

_____ **3.** Is it appropriate to give a gift at a wedding?

_____ **4.** Is it possible to appropriate land?

_____ **5.** Ada took Lin's ID and then gave it back. Did she appropriate it?

_____ **6.** The government did not vote to use more money for housing. Did the government appropriate the money?

C Follow the directions below. Write your answers on the lines.

1. List two things that are **appropriate** to wear to school.

   _____

   _____

2. List two things that the government should **appropriate** more

   money for.

   _____

   _____

Lesson 6 Wrap-up

 ## Talk About It

Discuss questions 1–5 with a partner.

Topic:
How music affects my life

Details:

1. Why do you think music in the United States is so **diverse**?

2. What kind of music do you think would be **appropriate** for a school dance?

3. How would you like to **expand** your collection of music?

4. What **aspect** of music do you enjoy the most?

5. How does music **enhance** your life?

 ## Write About It

Write about music on the lines below. Use ideas from Talk About It.

Topic:
Music affects my life because _____

_____.

Details:

1. Music in the United States is very diverse because _____

_____.

2. I think the kind of music that would be appropriate

   for a school dance is _____

_____.

3. I would like to expand my collection of music with _____

_____.

4. The aspect of music I enjoy most is _____

_____.

5. Music enhances my life by _____

_____.

Unit 2 Wrap-up

 Think About It

Think about the words you learned in Unit 2. Have you mastered them? Write each word under the right heading: Words I Have Mastered or Words I Need to Review. Make sentences using the words to prepare for the Unit Assessment.

Vocabulary Words

appropriate	expand
aspect	flexible
diverse	incorporate
enhance	transform
evolve	unique

Words I Have Mastered

_____   _____

_____   _____

_____   _____

_____   _____

_____   _____

Words I Need to Review

_____   _____

_____   _____

_____   _____

Practice Sentences

_____

_____

_____

_____

_____

_____

_____

_____

Unit 2 Assessment

A **Read these letters to the editor from two different students.**
Circle the word that completes each sentence.

TO THE EDITOR:

   I agree with your well-written story about music. An important

(**unique, aspect**) of music is how it makes a person feel. Each

person has (**evolve, unique**) feelings about music. Music can

(**diverse, transform**) a person's life. Your story also points out that

music can (**appropriate, enhance**) a person's experiences. The

story made me want to (**expand, aspect**) my knowledge of music.

Thank you for your inspiring work!

Sincerely,
Arturo

Write a word from the box to complete each sentence.

appropriate	diverse	evolve	flexible	incorporate

TO THE EDITOR:

   Your article about rock music stated that rock fans have

(1) _____ opinions. Here is my opinion. I think

that rock music will (2) _____ over time, but

it will always be exciting. Rock can (3) _____

different styles, such as hip-hop and blues. There's nothing wrong

with mixing. I think mixing styles is (4) _____.

My musical taste is (5) _____. Is yours?

Sincerely,
Weiyin

B Circle the letter of the answer that best completes each sentence.

1. A card is an _____ way to thank someone.
   a. unique
   b. appropriate
   c. diverse

2. I will _____ her chart into my plan.
   a. incorporate
   b. insight
   c. indoors

3. Gorillas make an amazing _____ when they grow from babies to adults.
   a. transformation
   b. transformer
   c. transform

4. The actor _____ an idea from another television show.
   a. reacted
   b. appropriated
   c. accompanied

C Circle the letter of the answer that means the same thing as the underlined word or phrase.

1. Talking is not appropriate behavior in a quiet movie theater.
   a. legal
   b. correct
   c. disappointing

2. It was so cold outside that we had to go indoors.
   a. through many doors
   b. into a building
   c. under a tree

3. The lights went out because of damaged wires in a transformer.
   a. device related to steam
   b. device related to water
   c. device related to electricity

4. The reporter interviewed people to gain an insight into the town.
   a. a tape-recording of
   b. a fear of
   c. an understanding of

D For each item, write a sentence that uses both words.

1. transform, unique

   _____

   _____

2. expand, flexible

   _____

   _____

3. appropriate, diverse

   _____

   _____

What Makes a Good Friend?

Vocabulary
- colleague
- compatible
- compensate
- distribute
- evaluate
- exceed
- mutual
- status
- transport
- undertake

Word Study
- The Root *port*
- Collocations
- Word Forms

"Friends have a lot to talk about. They pass the time together. Friends always treat you like you are the best. They tease you in a good way and help you grow up."

Daivaashish is from India.

Vocabulary in Context

Look at the photos and read the text. Respond to the text.

Dog owners may have small dogs, large dogs, indoor dogs, or outdoor dogs. People choose dogs to match their personalities. Someone who likes to run around outside will be **compatible** with an active dog. A person who likes staying indoors may be compatible with a "lap dog."

What kind of dog would you be compatible with?

To get a dog is to **undertake** a big challenge. A dog owner takes on the responsibility to feed and care for the animal. Owners must sometimes take their dogs to a veterinarian. And they may need special cages to **transport** their pets.

Describe the picture.

Despite the responsibility, owning a dog has many benefits. There are so many benefits that they can **exceed** the challenges pet owners face. The companionship of a dog can **compensate** for all of the hard work. Many owners believe the reward is worth the effort.

What other benefits can dogs offer?

Definitions

Read the definitions and example sentences.

compatible (kəm-pa′-tə-bəl)

adjective able to exist or function well with another

The friends are **compatible** because they share an interest in space.

compensate (käm′-pən-sāt′)

verb to make up for

I will **compensate** for burning the chicken by cooking a new one.

exceed (ik-sēd′)

verb to go beyond the limit of

The weight of the suitcase must not **exceed** forty pounds.

transport (trans-pôrt′)

verb to carry from one place to another

The trucks **transport** the apples to grocery stores.

undertake (ən′-dər-tāk′)

verb to take responsibility for; to attempt

The students will **undertake** a project to clean up the beach.

Choose one word to draw in this space.

Definitions Check

A Write the word from the box that matches the two examples in each item.

compatible	compensate	exceed	transport	undertake

1. _____
best friends
a computer and its printer

2. _____
to start to paint a room
to begin an assignment

3. _____
to go faster than the speed limit
to talk for too long in a debate

4. _____
to move boxes to a new home
to carry books to school

B Write the word from the box that relates to each group of words.

compatible	compensate	exceed	transport	undertake

_____ **1.** make up for, repay, balance

_____ **2.** fit, harmony, together

_____ **3.** move, carry

_____ **4.** beat, outdo, go beyond

_____ **5.** try, attempt

C Write the word from the box that answers each question.

compatible	compensate	exceed	transport	undertake

1. Which word goes with *to carry groceries home*? _____

2. Which word goes with *work well together*? _____

3. Which word goes with *to use crutches to walk*? _____

4. Which word goes with *to agree to oversee a project*? _____

5. Which word goes with *to drive faster than the limit*? _____

This rescue dog is at the scene of a disaster.

Friends and Rescuers

When a disaster like a hurricane or a tornado occurs, people rush to help those affected by it. Sometimes dogs help too. These rescue dogs **undertake** many types of missions. For example, they search for people who are buried during an earthquake or stuck in a mudslide. The dogs' owners **transport** them to the emergency area. An owner may drive for several hours to take a dog to a collapsed building or a train wreck.

What do you think the rescue is dog doing in this picture?

Dogs are intelligent animals by nature, and rescue dogs also receive up to two years of training. To work well as a team, the owner and the dog must be **compatible.** The training goes better when they enjoy being together. Owners expect a lot from their dogs, and the dogs usually **exceed** the owners' expectations. Dogs can save lives.

Despite spending hundreds of hours training their dogs, owners don't feel cheated. They feel **compensated** for their hard work by their rescue dogs' loyalty and bravery during dangerous situations.

How are the owner and the dog able to become a powerful team?

Comprehension Check

A Write T if the sentence is true. Write F if the sentence is false.

_____ 1. Rescue dogs often **exceed** their owners' expectations.

_____ 2. Owners **undertake** the work of rescuing people with their dogs.

_____ 3. The owners are **compensated** with money from the government.

_____ 4. Rescue dogs and their owners should be **compatible**.

_____ 5. Rescue dogs are trained to **transport** food to other animals.

B Write the word from the box that completes each sentence.

compatible	compensate	exceed	transport	undertake

Rescue dogs often (1) _____ the expectations of their

owners. The owners (2) _____ the mission of finding

people during emergencies. Owners (3) _____

rescue dogs to a location. Owners and rescue dogs must be

(4) _____. A dog's friendship and abilities

(5) _____ for the owner's hard work.

C Write the word from the box that replaces the underlined words.

compatible	compensates	exceeds	transport	undertake

_____ 1. Friendship with a dog <u>makes up</u> for the owner's work.

_____ 2. Rescue training <u>is more than</u> normal training.

_____ 3. Rescue dogs should be <u>able to work well together</u> with police and other emergency workers.

_____ 4. All pet owners <u>take responsibility for</u> the project of caring for and training their animals.

_____ 5. It may be difficult to <u>move</u> a large animal.

Word Study The Root *port*

The root of a word is the part that tells us the basic meaning of the word. The root *port* comes from the Latin word *portare*, which means "to carry." Some words that are built from this root are *transport*, *export*, and *portable.*

Word	Root	Meaning
transport		to carry across or from one place to another
export	*port* = to carry	to carry or send something out of the country for sale or trade
portable		capable of being carried

1 *export* (*ex* + *port*)

The prefix *ex-* can mean "out" or "out of." **Export** is a verb that means "to send something for sale or trade to another place or country."

The United States can <u>send out</u> products to other countries.

Florida will <u>send out</u> oranges to other states.

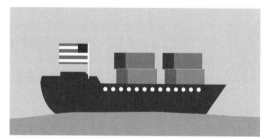

The United States can **export** products to other countries.

Florida will **export** oranges to other states.

2 *portable* (*port* + *able*)

The suffix *-able* means "able to be" or "that can be."
Portable is an adjective that means "capable of being carried."

The radio is <u>able to be carried</u> because it is not too heavy.

The new mug made her morning tea <u>able to be carried</u>.

The radio is **portable** because it is not too heavy.

The new mug made her morning tea **portable.**

Word Study Check The Root *port*

A **For each word, circle the root.**

Example: air(port)

1. transport

2. export

3. portable

B **Circle the word that completes each sentence.**

Holland and Peru (**export, portable**) flowers to other countries. Trucks

(**transport, export**) the flowers to stores. The workers in the stores

put flowers into light, (**transported, portable**) boxes and vases for

their customers.

C **Complete each sentence.**

1. People use trucks to transport _____

_____.

2. The United States exports _____

_____.

3. An example of something portable is _____

_____.

D **Circle the word that has a very different meaning from the other three words in its row.**

1. carry   move   transport   think

2. portable   lightweight   readable   movable

3. send   hold   export   deliver

Lesson 7 Wrap-up

Talk About It

Discuss questions 1–5 with a partner.

Topic:
What makes a good friend

Details:

1. How do you **undertake** the goal of being a good friend?

2. How important is it to be **compatible** with a good friend?

3. If you were **transported** to an island, what person or pet would you like to join you? Why?

4. How do you **compensate** a friend for helping you?

5. What do you expect from a friend? When has a friend **exceeded** this?

Write About It

Write about what makes a good friend on the lines below. Use ideas from Talk About It.

Topic:
Being a good friend means _____

_____.

Details:

1. I undertake the goal of being a good friend by _____

_____.

2. Some people think being compatible with a good friend is

important. I think _____

_____.

3. If I were transported to an island, I would take _____

because _____.

4. When a friend helps me, I compensate that friend by _____

_____.

5. A time a friend exceeded my expectations was when _____

_____

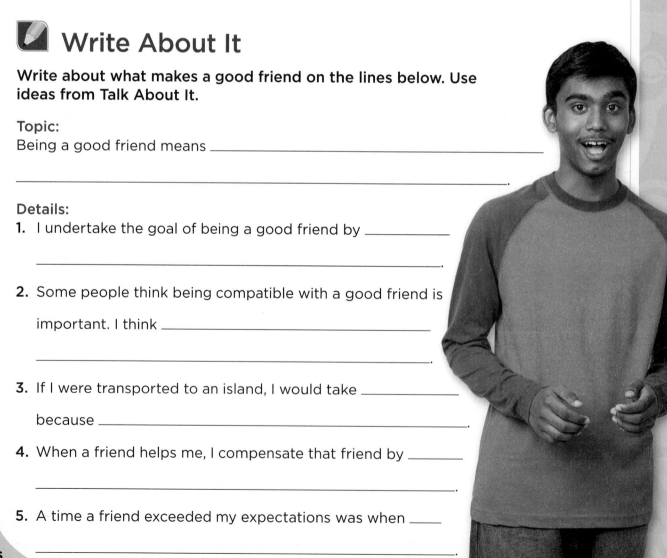

66

Vocabulary in Context

Look at the photos and read the text. Respond to the text.

Everyone needs friends to talk to and **undertake** projects with. When friends attempt a project and reach a goal together, their friendship grows stronger.

True friends go out of their way to help each other. Friends **exceed** what average people will do for one another. How are the friends in the picture helping each other?

How can someone new in town make friends?

If a person has a favorite pastime or sport, he or she can join a club or team that shares their interest. People with **mutual** interests often become friends.

A person with a job may become friends with a **colleague.** A teacher may become friends with another teacher or the principal. A principal has more authority at the school than a teacher, but people do not need equal **status** at their jobs in order to be friends.

Who is another colleague a teacher may have?

Definitions

Read the definitions and example sentences.

colleague (kä'-lēg)

noun someone who works in the same place or at the same type of job

At work Jorge sits next to his **colleague,** Marsha.

exceed (ik-sēd')

verb to go beyond the limit of

I worry that Bonkers will **exceed** the weight limit for a healthy cat.

mutual (mū'-chōō-əl)

adjective something shared between two or more people or things

Yesterday Luisa and Marta found out they have a **mutual** friend.

status (sta'-təs)

noun a person or thing's position in relation to others

The blue ribbon shows the painting's **status** in the art contest.

undertake (ən'-dər-tāk')

verb to take responsibility for; to attempt

The sisters will **undertake** the project of repainting their bedroom.

Choose one word to draw in this space.

Definitions Check

A **Match the beginning of each sentence with its ending.**

_____ 1. I see my colleague   **a.** five pages.

_____ 2. The essay may not exceed   **b.** when I go to work.

_____ 3. They have a mutual   **c.** higher than the mayor's.

_____ 4. The president's status is   **d.** the job of raising money.

_____ 5. The club will undertake   **e.** friend at school.

B **Put a check by the sentence that uses the bold word correctly.**

_____ 1. My **colleague** will present the data to our boss.

_____   My brother is the oldest **colleague** in the family.

_____ 2. Her cake will **exceed** what the judges expected.

_____   She will remove the **exceed** frosting from the cake.

_____ 3. All the team members wore **mutual** uniforms.

_____   All the team members had the **mutual** goal of winning.

_____ 4. The coach has a higher **status** than the players.

_____   The tallest player on the team is taller in **status** than the coach.

_____ 5. Lin will **undertake** the goal of finishing the book today.

_____   Lin will **undertake** all of the vegetables from the garden.

C **Circle the answer to each question. The answer is in the question. The first one has been done for you.**

1. Is a (person) or a computer an example of a _colleague_?

2. Will the box _exceed_ the weight limit if it is too heavy or too light?

3. If friends have a _mutual_ interest in music, do they share it or ignore it?

4. Who has the higher _status_ on a ship, the captain or a sailor?

5. Do you _undertake_ a tree or a mission?

Cesar Chavez and Fred Ross were friends and colleagues.

The Power of Friendship

When Cesar Chavez worked as a migrant farm worker in California, farm owners would hire migrant workers at a certain rate of pay and then pay them less. Workers would pick full boxes of vegetables, but the owner would pay them for less. These workers had low status in the community. They had to sit in separate sections of theaters and were discriminated against in other ways. What else have you learned about people discriminating against others?

Chavez decided to help farm workers fight for their rights. He learned to organize workers from Fred Ross, who worked for the Community Service Organization (CSO). Chavez and Ross met in 1952. At first, Chavez did not trust Ross, who was not Latino or a farm worker. Soon, Chavez saw that he and Ross had the mutual goal of improving the lives of the farm workers.

The two men became colleagues at the CSO. Ross asked Chavez to undertake a drive to register farm workers to vote. That year the number of new voters in San Jose, California, exceeded six thousand. Chavez and Ross remained close friends throughout their lives.

What other outcomes do you think came from their work?

Comprehension Check

A Write T if the sentence is true. Write F if the sentence is false.

_____ 1. Chavez and Ross had a **mutual** goal.

_____ 2. Farm workers in California had a high **status** in their communities.

_____ 3. Chavez and Ross planned to **undertake** a drive to register voters.

_____ 4. In 1952 the number of new voters did not **exceed** a few hundred.

_____ 5. Ross and Chavez were **colleagues** at a university.

B Write the word from the box that completes each sentence.

colleagues	exceeded	mutual	status	undertake

Chavez and Ross were (1) _____ at the CSO.

They chose to (2) _____ the project of helping

Latinos become voters. The number of new voters in San Jose

(3) _____ six thousand that year. They helped

migrant workers improve their (4) _____ in society.

They had the (5) _____ goal of helping people.

C Write the word from the box that replaces the underlined words.

colleagues	exceeded	mutual	status	undertake

_____ 1. Many migrant farm workers had the <u>shared</u> goal of wanting to end discrimination.

_____ 2. Chavez and Ross were <u>people who worked together</u>.

_____ 3. Changing your <u>position related to others</u> can be hard.

_____ 4. Chavez and Ross decided to <u>attempt</u> a project together even though it was a challenge.

_____ 5. Chavez may have <u>gone beyond</u> what people expected him to do during his life.

Word Study Collocations

A collocation is a phrase or group of words that people use a lot. Read about two collocations that use the word *status*. They have different meanings.

1 *status quo:* **the way things usually are or have always been**
- The status quo at our school is that students must share lockers.
- You can change the status quo by joining the student government.

Snowy weather is the status quo for winter in the North.

At the farmer's market, bringing your own bag is the status quo.

2 *status symbol:* **something a person owns or does that shows his or her status**
- Willy's fancy shoes are a status symbol because they show his wealth.
- Hilda thinks that her college degree is a status symbol.

To many people, gold jewelry is a status symbol.

Owning a large yacht is a status symbol that impresses some people.

Word Study Check Collocations

A Rewrite each sentence on the line below it. Replace the underlined words with a collocation from the box.

status quo	status symbol

1. A wrestling trophy is a <u>thing that shows status</u> among my friends.

   _____

2. The <u>way things usually are</u> in the library is that it is quiet.

   _____

3. The <u>way things have always been</u> at our meetings is that they are long.

   _____

B Circle the word that does not belong with the others in its row. The first one is done for you.

1. status quo for a healthy diet:

   fruit   (cookies)   vegetables   water

2. status symbol among athletes:

   trophy   ribbon   medal   pencil

3. status quo for a school day:

   classes   teachers   parade   lunch

C Complete the sentences below.

1. A status symbol among my friends is _____.

2. One way the status quo of my school should change is _____

   _____.

3. In many countries, a status symbol is _____.

4. A status symbol for my parents would be _____.

5. The status quo for dinner at my house is _____.

Lesson 8 Wrap-up

 Talk About It

Discuss questions 1–5 with a partner.

Topic:
Different ways of making friends

Details:

1. Is it important for friends to have **mutual** interests? Why or why not?

2. How could a **colleague** at work become a friend?

3. Do you expect to be close with new friends? Do you ever **exceed** that?

4. What plan could you **undertake** to make a friend at school?

5. How do you become friends with a person with a different **status**?

Write About It

Write about making friends on the lines below. Use ideas from Talk About It.

Topic:
There are many ways to make friends. Some of these are _____

_____.

Details:

1. Some people think it is important for friends to have mutual

   interests. I believe _____

   _____.

2. A colleague at work could become a friend if _____

   _____.

3. I expect to be close to a friend _____.

   A time I exceeded that was _____.

4. A plan I could undertake to make a friend at school is _____

   _____.

5. I could become friends with someone with different status by

   _____.

74

Vocabulary in Context

Look at the photos and read the text. Respond to the text.

Many schools sponsor clubs for students interested in everything from architecture to zoology. Before you join a club, you should examine and judge the club's goals and activities. You can also **evaluate** a club's members to see if you will work well with them. It is important to find people you are **compatible** with.

What clubs have you thought about joining?

The work of a club is shared. If a club wants to put on a musical event, some members make fliers to announce it. Others **distribute** the fliers by handing them out to people. Still others **transport** music equipment from the school to the event location.

What is happening in this picture?

Clubs offer a chance for you to meet people who care about the same things you do. Your **mutual** interests can help form long-lasting friendships.

What interests do you share with your friends?

Definitions

Read the definitions and example sentences.

compatible (kəm-pa′-tə-bəl)

adjective able to exist or function well with another

My best friend and I are **compatible** because we both love the outdoors.

distribute (di-stri′-būt)

verb to deliver or give out to several people or groups

My job is to **distribute** the shirts to everybody on the team.

evaluate (i-val′-ū-āt′)

verb to examine and judge carefully

He will **evaluate** each toy to make sure it is safe.

mutual (mū′-chōō-əl)

adjective something shared between two or more people or things

My friend and I have a **mutual** interest in biking.

transport (trans-pôrt′)

verb to carry from one place to another

FROM FISH TO FERRET

I can **transport** the fish home from the pet store in a plastic bag.

Choose one word to draw in this space.

Definitions Check

A Put a check by the answer to each question.

1. Which sentence is an example of two people who are compatible?
   _____ My brother and I always argue when we skateboard together.
   _____ My brother and I laugh and talk when we skateboard together.

2. Which sentence is about someone who plans to transport something?
   _____ I will carry the books to the library.
   _____ I will arrange the books on the library shelf.

3. Which sentence is an example of someone who wants to distribute something?
   _____ I will borrow a pencil from a student.
   _____ I will give a pencil to each student.

4. Which sentence is an example of something that is mutual?
   _____ Marco listens to the music only because Amina enjoys it.
   _____ Marco and Amina both enjoy listening to music.

B Write the word from the box that completes each sentence.

compatible	distribute	evaluate	mutual	transport

1. Friends who get along well are _____.

2. Before I decide, I will _____ all the choices.

3. The bus driver can _____ us to the museum.

4. I will _____ snacks to the other students.

5. We have a _____ dislike of bananas.

C Complete the sentences below.

1. My friend and I have a mutual interest in _____.

2. I often evaluate _____.

3. Our teacher plans to distribute _____.

4. I am compatible with people who _____.

5. Sometimes I must transport _____.

A teen volunteer reads to younger children.

Teens Make Friends with Their Libraries

Teens across the United States have become friends with their libraries. These teens have joined volunteer clubs, such as Teen Friends of the Library, that promote reading and books in their communities. The friends of libraries and the employees of libraries have a **mutual** goal. Both groups want to get young people excited about reading. How do you think they achieve this goal?

Teen volunteers entertain younger children by reading mysteries and adventure stories to them. Volunteers also invite famous authors to their libraries to talk to students in person. Another mutual goal of libraries and their friends is to make good books available to everyone. Teen volunteers work to achieve this goal by **distributing** used books to people. If people in the community have trouble traveling to the library, volunteers help by **transporting** books to and from people's homes.

Some teen library groups also help **evaluate** new books. Volunteers read recently published books and then write reports telling what each book was about. If they report that a book is interesting and challenging, the library will often order more copies.

Teen volunteers and libraries are **compatible**—they go together well! What can you do for your local library?

Comprehension Check

A   **Write T if the sentence is true. Write F if the sentence is false.**

_____ 1. Some teen library groups **evaluate** new books.

_____ 2. Teen library clubs and libraries have a **mutual** goal.

_____ 3. Libraries and teen library groups are not very **compatible**.

_____ 4. Libraries **distribute** money to teen volunteers.

_____ 5. Some teen library groups **transport** books to people.

B   **Write the word from the box that completes each sentence.**

compatible	distributing	evaluating	mutual	transport

Teens and library workers are (1) _____ because

they have a (2) _____ goal. They want people to

use the library. Teen library groups (3) _____

books to people who are not able to leave their homes. Teens also help

by (4) _____ used books to readers and by

(5) _____ new books.

C   **Write the word from the box that replaces the underlined words.**

compatible	distribute	evaluate	mutual	transport

_____ 1. Not all teens are <u>able to get along well</u>.

_____ 2. Teens who are not old enough to drive may use their bicycles to <u>move</u> books.

_____ 3. Teens <u>carefully judge</u> ways to help their communities.

_____ 4. Some libraries <u>give out</u> awards and prizes to volunteers to reward their hard work.

_____ 5. Many teens have a <u>common or shared</u> interest in reading new books.

Word Study Word Forms

Words often have several different forms. Read below about some of the different word forms of *distribute.*

1 *distribution* (noun)

Distribution is the act of giving out or delivering something.

Volunteers help **distribute** books to children.

Volunteers help with the **distribution** of books to children.

I **distributed** food at the homeless shelter for two hours.

The **distribution** of the food at the homeless shelter lasted for two hours.

2 *distributor* (noun)

A person who gives out or delivers something is a *distributor.*

Jinhee will **distribute** pencils to everyone in class today.

Jinhee will be the pencil **distributor** in class today.

He **distributes** newspapers to all the houses on our block.

He is the newspaper **distributor** for the houses on our block.

Word Study Check Word Forms

A **Circle the word that completes each sentence.**

Lee will (**distribute, distributor**) the toys to the children. He will be the

(**distribution, distributor**) of the toys. The (**distribution, distributor**) of

the toys will last for three hours.

B **Complete each sentence.**

1. I once distributed _____

_____.

2. I participate in the distribution of _____

_____.

3. I once was the distributor of _____

_____.

C **Match each word to its meaning.**

_____ 1. distribute   **a.** to deliver

_____ 2. distribution   **b.** someone who delivers

_____ 3. distributor   **c.** the act of delivering

D **Write the word from the box that completes each sentence.**

distribute	distribution	distributors

1. You can _____ one book to each child.

2. Please help the other book _____ hand out
   the extra books.

3. The _____ of books is an important activity.

Lesson 9 Wrap-up

 ## Talk About It

Discuss questions 1–5 with a partner.

Topic:
Joining clubs

Details:

1. Are members of a club always compatible? Why or why not?

2. How can mutual interests help people become friends?

3. How can you evaluate a club to see if it is right for you?

4. What things might a club leader distribute to members? Why?

5. What kinds of things would a leader transport to club events?

Write About It

Write about joining a club on the lines below. Use ideas from Talk About It.

Topic:
Joining a club can be a good way to make friends because _____

_____.

Details:

1. Members of a club may be compatible because _____

_____. They may not be compatible because

_____.

2. Mutual interests help people to become friends because

_____.

3. Before joining a club, I would evaluate it by _____

_____.

4. The leader of a club might distribute _____

to members because _____.

5. A leader may need to transport _____

_____ to club meetings and events.

Unit 3 Wrap-up

 Think About It

Think about the words you learned in Unit 3. Have you mastered them? Write each word under the right heading: Words I Have Mastered or Words I Need to Review. Make sentences using the words to prepare for the Unit Assessment.

Vocabulary Words

colleague   exceed
compatible   mutual
compensate   status
distribute   transport
evaluate   undertake

Words I Have Mastered

_____   _____

_____   _____

_____   _____

_____   _____

Words I Need to Review

_____   _____

_____   _____

_____   _____

Practice Sentences

_____

_____

_____

_____

_____

_____

_____

_____

_____

Unit 3 Assessment

A Read the postcards sent between Daivaashish and Hector.

Circle the word that completes each sentence.

Hi, Hector,

I'm with my father in St. Louis. He is here to (**compensate, evaluate**) plans for a new medical center. Today I met some of his (**colleagues, statuses**). They are quite (**compatible, compensate**) with one another. My father respects them a lot, and the feeling is (**exceed, mutual**).

Sorry I couldn't go to your party. I'll bring you something from St. Louis to (**compensate, exceed**) for it.

Your friend,
Daivaashish

Hector Ruiz
123 Center St.
Your Town,
Your State
12345

Write a word from the box to complete each sentence.

| distribute | exceed | status | transport | undertake |

Hi, Daivaashish! It's cool that your father has a job with such a high (1) _____. People need his opinion to (2) _____ a new project! I bet his advice will (3) _____ their expectations. How will they (4) _____ the medical equipment to the new place?

Coach Jim is going to (5) _____ T-shirts to the team on Friday. Will you be back by then?

Your Friend,
Hector

Daivaashish
Hotel H
St. Louis,
Missouri 54321

B Circle the letter of the answer that best completes each sentence.

1. Things must change. I do not accept the _____.
   a. status
   b. status symbol
   c. status quo

2. She works as a makeup _____.
   a. distribute
   b. distribution
   c. distributor

3. Mexico _____ mangos to other countries.
   a. exports
   b. expands
   c. experiences

4. As president, Sanjay has a high _____ in the club.
   a. status
   b. status symbol
   c. status quo

C Circle the letter of the answer that means the same thing as the underlined word or phrase.

1. He wears expensive clothes as a status symbol.
   a. way to take away his status
   b. way to show his status
   c. way to hide his status

2. When I go camping, I cook with a portable stove.
   a. stove that can be carried
   b. stove that cannot be lost
   c. stove that heats food

3. We need volunteers to help with the distribution of the supplies.
   a. colleague
   b. delivery
   c. aspect

4. Who is going to transport the costumes to the theater?
   a. share
   b. carry
   c. offer

D For each item, write a sentence that uses both words.

1. compatible, mutual

   _____

   _____

2. exceed, undertake

   _____

   _____

3. colleague, evaluate

   _____

   _____

What Makes Me Healthy?

Vocabulary
alternative
attain
concentrate
external
indicate
internal
objective
promote
significant
substitute

Word Study
- Word Forms
- Multiple Meanings
- Collocations

"Health is about striking a balance. For example, my family's homemade food is delicious, but it can be fatty. So I eat a healthy breakfast."

Adrian is from Mexico.

Vocabulary in Context

Look at the photos and read the text. Respond to the text.

To have a healthy body, you need to do good things for it. You exercise and eat nutritious food. You should also **concentrate** on your mental health. Your mind and your emotions need attention too. Studies show that students often feel *stress*, a strain on the brain.

What causes stress for you?

Studies also **indicate** that stress can cause health problems. Some of the most **significant** problems include anxiety, headaches, and depression. To fight stress, you should get enough sleep, break tasks into small steps, and talk about your worries.

How else can you deal with stress?

Stress can affect your **external** appearance. People often know when you are feeling stress just by looking at you. When your stress level is lower, you will be healthier on the inside as well. Your **internal** organs, such as your heart, will work better.

Why is being healthy important?

Definitions

Read the definitions and example sentences.

concentrate (kän′-sən-trāt′)

verb to focus or center your attention on something

Chess players must **concentrate** on where the pieces are.

external (ek-stər′-nəl)

adjective on the outside

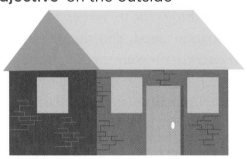

The **external** part of the house is made mostly of brick.

indicate (in′-də-kāt′)

verb to point out or show

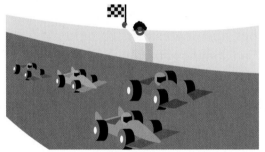

Sara waved a flag to **indicate** that the race was over.

internal (in-tər′-nəl)

adjective on the inside

Your heart is one of your **internal** organs.

significant (sig-ni′-fi-kənt)

adjective important; meaningful; noteworthy

The difference in their heights is **significant.**

Choose one word to draw in this space.

Definitions Check

A Write the word from the box that matches the two examples in each item.

| concentrate | external | indicate | internal | significant |

1. _____
a trip that affected you deeply
the lesson that made the difference

2. _____
secret papers of the government
a problem inside the stomach

3. _____
to show where a place is
to point to the one you want

4. _____
to think hard about a math problem
to focus on winning a game

B Write the word from the box that relates to each group of words.

| concentrate | external | indicate | internal | significant |

_____ **1.** tell, show, say

_____ **2.** think, focus, study

_____ **3.** hair, fingernails, skin

_____ **4.** huge, crucial, meaningful

_____ **5.** heart, lungs, brain

C Write the word from the box that answers each question.

| concentrate | external | indicate | internal | significant |

1. Which word goes with *how you feel*? _____

2. Which word goes with *how you look*? _____

3. Which word goes with *to focus on solving a puzzle*? _____

4. Which word goes with *the main point*? _____

5. Which word goes with *the hands of a clock*? _____

Many teens do not get enough sleep.

Teens, Sleep, and Health

Do you get enough sleep? If you said "no," you are not alone. Research **indicates** that many teens do not sleep enough. Most adolescents sleep fewer than eight hours each night. Experts estimate that adolescents should sleep at least nine hours.

Not sleeping enough has many **significant** effects. Teens may feel drowsy, have difficulty **concentrating,** or show poor judgment. They might not perform very well on tests. Lack of sleep can make it harder to play team sports or to participate in clubs after school. What other problems could you have if you did not get enough sleep?

Experts say that the **internal** "body clocks" of adolescents are part of the reason they don't get enough sleep. Their bodies tell them to be active at the times when they should be sleeping. It is not easy to adjust your internal body clock. But sleep experts believe that you can change your sleep cycle. First, go to bed at the same time every night and turn off all the lights in the room. Block **external** light and sound as much as possible.

What else can you do to sleep well?

Comprehension Check

A **Write T if the sentence is true. Write F if the sentence is false.**

_____ 1. It is hard to **concentrate** on your studies without sleep.

_____ 2. Studies **indicate** that most teens get too much sleep.

_____ 3. **External** sounds will help you sleep better.

_____ 4. Not getting enough sleep may harm teens in **significant** ways.

_____ 5. Teens' **internal** body clocks can cause them to lose sleep.

B **Write the word from the box that completes each sentence.**

concentrating	external	indicate	internal	significant

Studies show that a (1) _____ number of teens do not sleep

enough. These studies (2) _____ that teens have problems

as a result. They might have a difficult time (3) _____.

Teens need to set their (4) _____ body clocks.

Controlling (5) _____ noises and turning off lights will

help them get to sleep earlier.

C **Write the word from the box that replaces the underlined words.**

concentrate	external	indicate	internal	significant

1. _____ Puffy eyes <u>show</u> that a teen needs more sleep.

2. _____ Not getting enough sleep is a <u>major</u> problem for many teens.

3. _____ You may be kept awake at night by <u>outside</u> factors.

4. _____ Some <u>inner</u> problems may affect how well you sleep.

5. _____ Some researchers want to <u>center their attention</u> on solving the sleep problem.

Word Study Word Forms

Words often have several different forms. Read below about some of the different word forms of *significant*.

1 *significance* (noun)

If something has *significance*, it has importance or meaning.

Her research was **significant** because it led to a new medicine.

The **significance** of her research was that it led to a new medicine.

The battle of Bunker Hill was a **significant** event in our history.

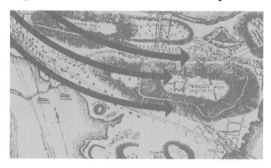

The battle of Bunker Hill has historical **significance** for us.

2 *signify* (verb)

To *signify* is to mean, show, or represent.

Jesse's nod is **significant** because it means that he is on my side.

Jesse nods to **signify** that he is on my side.

In a Korean wedding, the color red is **significant**. It means happiness.

In a Korean wedding, the color red has meaning. It **signifies** happiness.

Word Study Check Word Forms

A **Circle the word that completes each sentence.**

All of Dr. Soto's research is (**significant, signify**). His biggest study has the

most (**signify, significance**) because it led to a new medicine. Dr. Soto's

many awards (**significant, signify**) that he is a successful scientist.

B **Complete each sentence.**

1. The most significant event I can remember is _____

_____.

2. To signify that I am bored, I _____

_____.

3. An object in my home that has great significance to me is _____

_____.

C **Match each word to its meaning.**

_____ 1. signify   **a.** important or meaningful

_____ 2. significance   **b.** to mean, show, or represent

_____ 3. significant   **c.** importance or meaning

D **Write the word from the box that completes each sentence.**

significance   significant   signify

1. You will probably have many _____ events in
your life.

2. The astronaut's medals and awards _____ her
many accomplishments.

3. If something is not important to you, it has no _____.

Lesson 10 Wrap-up

 Talk About It

Discuss questions 1–5 with a partner.

Topic:
How a lack of sleep can affect my life

Details:

1. What are some signs that **indicate** you haven't had enough sleep?

2. Why is it important to be able to **concentrate** in school?

3. When does your **internal** body clock tell you to go to sleep?

4. Why is getting enough sleep **significant** to you?

5. How can you stop **external** noise from bothering you when you want to sleep?

 Write About It

Write about sleep on the lines below. Use ideas from Talk About It.

Topic:
A lack of sleep can affect my life because _____

_____.

Details:

1. Two signs that indicate I haven't had enough sleep are _____

_____.

2. It's important to concentrate in school because _____

_____.

3. My internal body clock tells me to go to sleep _____

_____.

4. To me, sleep is significant because _____

_____.

5. When external noise keeps me from falling asleep,

   I usually _____

_____.

Vocabulary in Context

Look at the photos and read the text. Respond to the text.

What is the main goal of a doctor? Some people say a doctor's main **objective** should be to cure people. During the past century, doctors have found many new ways to treat sick people. But another important objective is to prevent illness. What can doctors do to prevent illness?

New technology is helping doctors prevent illness. Technology can show a health problem in an early stage. For example, tests can **indicate** where cancer is beginning to grow. The tests make a big difference in a patient's treatment. The difference is so **significant** that it can save the patient's life.

Some ways of treating and preventing illness are different from traditional medicine. The practice of these methods is often called **alternative** medicine. It includes acupuncture, nutrition pills, and herbs. These methods **promote** health without drugs. Alternative medicine has improved many people's health. What kind of medicine do you prefer?

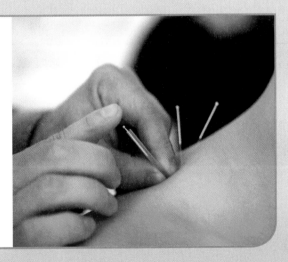

Definitions

Read the definitions and example sentences.

alternative (ôl-tər'-nə-tiv)

noun a different option; a choice between two or more things

One **alternative** to getting a job after school is joining a club.

indicate (in'-də-kāt')

verb to point out or show

The signs **indicate** that we should turn right to go to the airport.

objective (əb-jek'-tiv)

noun a goal or an aim

My **objective** is to run a marathon this summer.

promote (prə-mōt')

verb to aid or support the progress of something

Many parents **promote** music education in our school.

significant (sig-ni'-fi-kənt)

adjective important; meaningful; noteworthy

Kripa made a **significant** change to her bedroom wall when she painted it.

Choose one word to draw in this space.

Definitions Check

A Match the beginning of each sentence with its ending.

_____ 1. Her objective is

_____ 2. The votes indicate

_____ 3. The pep rally will promote

_____ 4. I made a significant

_____ 5. Riding the bus is an alternative

a. to walking.

b. change in my poem.

c. to go to college.

d. that Emerson has won.

e. school spirit.

B Put a check by the sentence that uses the bold word correctly.

_____ 1. Alice Walker is a **significant** author in my life.

_____ The house is in **significant** condition after the storm.

_____ 2. What is the **objective** of your experiment?

_____ From the plane, I had the **objective** of a bird.

_____ 3. The results **indicate** that he was successful.

_____ The orchestra will **indicate** music on the radio.

_____ 4. Her car won't start because the **alternative** doesn't work.

_____ I chose to walk as an **alternative** to riding.

_____ 5. This machine can **promote** raw fish and put it in cans.

_____ Our club will **promote** recycling at our school.

C Circle the answer to each question. The answer is in the question. The first one has been done for you.

1. Does a red stoplight _indicate_ go or (stop)?

2. Is a _significant_ change important or unimportant?

3. If you _promote_ an idea, do you let it die or support it?

4. Is an _alternative_ a choice or a prediction?

5. When you reach an _objective,_ do you meet a goal or give it up?

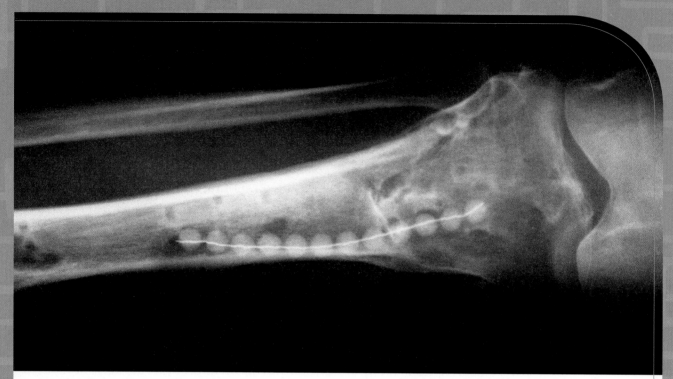

Antibiotic beads help cure infections.

Antibiotic Beads

Infections are concentrations of harmful bacteria. If you cut your finger, you need to cover it to prevent infection. In larger wounds, infections can cause **significant** problems—even death. Several generations ago, infections were a major cause of death in the United States. Today doctors use antibiotic medicine, which kills bacteria. They give this medicine in the form of shots or pills. But sometimes shots or pills cannot reach the wound fast enough. The blood carrying the antibiotics may leave the body instead of going to the wound.

An **alternative** to shots or pills is antibiotic beads. A doctor's **objective** when using these beads is to treat the infection faster. Doctors make antibiotic beads in the operating room by mixing the medicine with bone. They form the material into tiny round balls. The doctors put these beads on the open wound and the medicine moves right into the wound. Why do you think these beads **promote** faster healing?

When the infection is gone, doctors remove the beads and close the wound. Research **indicates** that wounds heal more quickly this way. Consequently patients need fewer operations. How could faster healing change the life of an athlete or a soldier?

Comprehension Check

A Write T if the sentence is true. Write F if the sentence is false.

_____ 1. Antibiotic beads are an **alternative** to shots.

_____ 2. One **objective** of doctors is to prevent illness.

_____ 3. Infections never cause **significant** problems.

_____ 4. Antibiotic beads **promote** slower healing.

_____ 5. Research **indicates** that antibiotic beads work well.

B Write the word from the box that completes each sentence.

alternative	indicate	objective	promote	significant

Antibiotic beads are an (1) _____ to shots and

pills. Tests (2) _____ that beads are better for

curing infections in a wound. They (3) _____ faster

healing. Doctors who use beads have the (4) _____

of avoiding future operations. Using the beads can make a

(5) _____ difference in how a patient heals.

C Write the word from the box that replaces the underlined words.

alternative	indicate	objective	promote	significant

_____ 1. The invention of antibiotic beads was <u>important</u>.

_____ 2. Antibiotics <u>aid</u> healing.

_____ 3. One <u>different choice</u> is to use antibiotic beads.

_____ 4. The doctors' <u>goal</u> is to speed healing.

_____ 5. Tests <u>show</u> that antibiotic beads are helpful.

Word Study Multiple Meanings

A word often has more than one meaning. Read about two different meanings of *objective.*

1 *objective:*   (noun) goal; aim
- my objective for today
- the objective of the fundraiser

- the objective of the game
- the objective of the math lesson

My objective is to reach the top of the mountain today.

The objective of the game is to make a touchdown.

2 *objective:*   (adjective) not influenced by personal opinions or feelings
- objective decision
- objective test

- objective statement
- objective evidence

A judge must be objective, making a decision based only on facts.

Ms. Oza says that being objective can help us learn facts about history, but it can't help us care about them.

Word Study Check Multiple Meanings

A For each numbered item, choose *a* or *b* as the correct meaning of the word in bold.

objective
a. (noun) goal; aim
b. (adjective) not influenced by personal opinions or feelings

1. _____ Mario tried to stay **objective** during his uncles' argument.

2. _____ Our **objective** is to collect 400 cans of food.

3. _____ What is your **objective** for summer school?

4. _____ I can't be **objective** about my family because I belong to it.

B Write "Yes" or "No" to answer each question.

_____ 1. Is a touchdown an objective in soccer?

_____ 2. Is one objective of a race to finish first?

_____ 3. Jim says our school should require uniforms because students look neater. Is that an objective statement?

_____ 4. Zoe based her decision on facts. Was she objective?

_____ 5. Bailey met a goal. Did she reach an objective?

_____ 6. Do people always meet their objectives?

C Follow the directions below. Write your answers on the lines.

1. List two things you might think about before you make an **objective** decision.

_____

_____

2. List two things you set **objectives** for.

_____

_____

Lesson 11 Wrap-up

 ## Talk About It

Discuss questions 1–5 with a partner.

Topic:
How doctors help people stay healthy

Details:

1. How can doctors **promote** good health?

2. What can different tests **indicate** about how healthy you are?

3. What is one **significant** improvement in medicine that you know about?

4. What is the **objective** of this improvement?

5. What new **alternatives** in medicine do you think might be available in the future?

 ## Write About It

Write about how doctors help people stay healthy on the lines below. Use ideas from Talk About It.

Topic:
Doctors help people stay healthy by _____
_____.

Details:

1. Doctors can promote good health by _____
_____.

2. Different medical tests can indicate _____
_____.

3. One significant improvement in medicine is _____
_____.

4. The objective of this improvement is _____
_____.

5. In the future, some medical alternatives might be _____
_____
_____.

Vocabulary in Context

Look at the photos and read the text. Respond to the text.

Most people want to be healthier. Is this one of your objectives? If you exercise, you are more likely to succeed. Exercise can help you **attain** your goal.

Exercise improves both your external appearance and your **internal** health. When you exercise, your body functions better on the inside.

Sports are a good form of exercise. You can play to win or just for fun. Sports **promote** good health.

If you don't like sports, you can **substitute** other activities for sports. You can take a walk or run on a treadmill. What kind of exercise do you prefer?

If you **concentrate** on the positive aspects of exercise, you will be more likely to do it. Pay attention to how good you feel when you exercise. Think of exercise as a part of your day, like school. How do you include exercise in your daily routine?

Definitions

Read the definitions and example sentences.

attain (ə-tān′)

verb to reach or arrive at; to accomplish

Reina worked hard to **attain** success at the science fair.

concentrate (kän′-sən-trāt′)

verb to focus or center your attention on something

If you **concentrate,** you can solve difficult math problems.

internal (in-tər′-nəl)

adjective on the inside

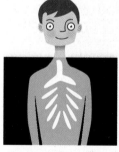

The x-ray shows that Paul has no **internal** injuries.

promote (prə-mōt′)

verb to aid or support the progress of something

These volunteers **promote** recycling by giving out information.

substitute (səb′-stə-tōōt′)

verb to put in the place of someone or something else

If you **substitute** cloth bags for plastic bags, you create less waste.

Choose one word to draw in this space.

Definitions Check

A Put a check by the answer to each question.

1. Which sentence is about something that someone can attain?
   _____ My sister weighed 7 pounds when she was born.
   _____ I got an A on the history test.

2. Which sentence is about something that is internal?
   _____ She broke a bone when she fell off her bike.
   _____ I could see a scratch on her knee after she fell.

3. Which sentence is about something someone can substitute?
   _____ He plans to use glue instead of tape to make his art project.
   _____ He plans to be on time to his art class starting today.

4. Which sentence was written by someone who cannot concentrate?
   _____ I am putting all my energy into wrestling practice.
   _____ I am having trouble thinking because of all the noise in the room.

B Write the word from the box that completes each sentence.

attain	concentrate	internal	promote	substitute

1. This company shreds its _____ papers.

2. Authors often travel to _____ their books.

3. I can _____ better when it is quiet.

4. The coach will _____ one of the players.

5. She tries to _____ excellence in her work.

C Complete the sentences below.

1. To promote school spirit, _____.

2. It is important to concentrate when _____.

3. My goal is to attain _____.

4. An example of an internal organ is _____.

5. You can substitute junk food with _____.

Teens exercise to stay in shape.

Teen Fitness Centers Promote Health

How fit are most teenagers? Most teens do not get enough exercise at home or at school. In an effort to **promote** good health among teenagers, fitness centers for young people have opened across the country.

Gyms for young people help teenagers **attain** a higher level of physical fitness. Unlike most other health clubs, these gyms have fitness machines and exercise classes designed for young people. These centers create an environment that students will want to return to day after day.

At fitness centers for teens, instructors teach students how to improve the way they exercise. Students learn to **concentrate** as they breathe, lift weights, and do other exercises. With the instructors' help, workouts are safer and more effective.

Nutrition classes teach students to **substitute** healthy snacks for junk food. Teenagers learn that their heart, lungs, and other **internal** organs will function better and longer if they exercise and eat right.

Joining a health club for teens is one of the ways a young person can get in shape. What else can young people do to improve their health?

Comprehension Check

A **Write T if the sentence is true. Write F if the sentence is false.**

_____ **1.** It is important to **concentrate** on physical fitness.

_____ **2.** Exercise can help you **attain** physical fitness.

_____ **3.** You can improve your **internal** health by eating well.

_____ **4.** Lack of exercise can **promote** good health.

_____ **5.** You should **substitute** junk food for healthy food.

B **Write the word from the box that completes each sentence.**

attain	concentrate	internal	promote	substitute

Exercise helps people (1) _____ physical fitness.

Teen gyms teach students to (2) _____ as they

exercise. They also teach students to (3) _____

healthy food for unhealthy food. Students learn that their

(4) _____ organs will benefit from exercise and a

balanced diet. They learn practices that (5) _____

long-term health.

C **Write the word or phrase from the box that replaces the underlined words.**

attain	concentrate	internal	promote	substitute for

_____ **1.** What can I drink instead of soda?

_____ **2.** Does milk contribute to good health?

_____ **3.** I want to focus more on my physical health.

_____ **4.** A good diet can help keep your inner organs healthy.

_____ **5.** A fitness center can help you reach your fitness goals.

Word Study Collocations

A collocation is a phrase or group of words that people use a lot. Below are two similar collocations that have an important difference. When you *substitute* A *for* B, you get A. When you *replace* A *with* B, you get B.

1 *substitute A for B:* to use A instead of B
- If you **substitute** water **for** soda at lunch, you can lose weight.
- The coach **substituted** Humberto **for** Tim in the second half.

You can **substitute** soybeans **for** meat to make a burger.

Kirit decided to **substitute** a sitar **for** the electric guitar in his band.

2 *replace A with B:* to use B instead of A
- If you **replace** soda **with** water at lunch, you can lose weight.
- The coach **replaced** Tim **with** Humberto in the second half.

The baker **replaced** his broken bowl **with** a new steel bowl.

If the phone you buy doesn't work, our company will **replace** it **with** a new one.

Word Study Check Collocations

A Rewrite each sentence on the line below it. Replace the underlined words with the collocation in parentheses.

1. (substitutes . . . for . . .)
If the dentist <u>uses</u> gold <u>instead of</u> silver, the tooth will last longer.

_____

2. (substituted . . . for . . .)
I <u>installed</u> a soft bike seat <u>in place of</u> my old hard seat.

_____

3. (replaced . . . with . . .)
The gardener <u>filled the place of</u> the dead tree <u>with</u> a fountain.

_____

B Write the group of words from the box that completes each sentence.

substitute for	replace with

When spring comes, you can (1) _____ a

sweater _____ a winter coat. When spring

becomes summer, you can (2) _____ the sweater

_____ a T-shirt.

Name two drinks you could substitute for soda in the summer.

1. _____   2. _____

C Complete the sentences below.

1. Ari replaced his old skateboard with a _____.

2. Mr. Jones replaced his fence with a _____.

3. Aurelia usually substitutes salads for _____.

4. You should never substitute money for _____.

Lesson 12 Wrap-up

 **Talk About It**

Discuss questions 1–5 with a partner.

Topic:
How to take care of my health

Details:

1. How can you **attain** good health over a lifetime?

2. What can you do to improve your **internal** health?

3. How do gyms **promote** physical fitness?

4. Why is it important to **concentrate** as you exercise?

5. To make your diet healthier, what would you **substitute** for fast food?

 Write About It

Write about health on the lines below. Use ideas from Talk About It.

Topic:
Taking care of my health is important because _____

_____.

Details:

1. I can attain good health by _____

_____.

2. I can improve my internal health by _____

_____.

3. Teen gyms promote physical fitness by _____

_____.

4. You should concentrate while you exercise because

_____.

5. To make my diet healthier, I would substitute _____

   for _____.

Unit 4 Wrap-up

 Think About It

Think about the words you learned in Unit 4. Have you mastered them? Write each word under the right heading: Words I Have Mastered or Words I Need to Review. Make sentences using the words to prepare for the Unit Assessment.

Vocabulary Words

alternative	internal
attain	objective
concentrate	promote
external	significant
indicate	substitute

Words I Have Mastered

_____ _____

_____ _____

_____ _____

_____ _____

_____ _____

Words I Need to Review

_____ _____

_____ _____

_____ _____

Practice Sentences

_____

_____

_____

_____

_____

_____

_____

_____

Unit 4 Assessment

A Read these letters to the editor from two different students.
Circle the word that completes each sentence.

TO THE EDITOR:

I agree that staying fit is a good (**objective, substitute**) to have.

They say that exercise is even good for (**external, internal**) organs.

There is no better (**objective, alternative**) for staying fit. But can

exercise really (**substitute, promote**) good mental health? I doubt

it. After I exercise in gym class, I still can't (**concentrate, promote**)

in math class.

Sincerely,
Luisa

Write a word from the box to complete each sentence.

attain	external	indicate	significant	substitute

TO THE EDITOR:

Your article states that people will be happy if they

(1) _____ good health. But many other

(2) _____ factors affect people's quality of life.

It won't bring me happiness just to (3) _____

one food for another. You also (4) _____

that exercise can make you look better on the outside. But

(5) _____ appearance is not the best way to

measure either health or happiness!

Sincerely,
Adrian

B Circle the letter of the answer that best completes each sentence.

1. You can be _____
   if you get the facts.
   a. objective
   b. internal
   c. significant

2. What is the _____
   of the scientist's discovery?
   a. signify
   b. significance
   c. significant

3. The _____ of the game
   is to score the most points.
   a. status
   b. colleague
   c. objective

4. I _____ the old pencil
   _____ a new one.
   a. replaced . . . with
   b. substituted . . . for
   c. incorporated . . . into

C Circle the letter of the answer that means the same thing as the
underlined word or phrase.

1. To make a new breakfast menu,
   Dan substituted oatmeal for eggs.
   a. ate oatmeal instead of eggs
   b. ate eggs instead of oatmeal
   c. ate oatmeal with eggs

2. There are significant differences
   between horses and deer.
   a. noticeable
   b. objective
   c. internal

3. In a fair trial, the judge must be
   objective.
   a. very focused on a goal
   b. influenced by an opinion
   c. not influenced by feelings

4. Raise your hand to signify
   that you understand.
   a. promote
   b. show
   c. offer

D For each item, write a sentence that uses both words.

1. concentrate, significant

   _____

   _____

2. external, internal

   _____

   _____

3. attain, indicate

   _____

   _____

What Can Journeys Teach?

"When I came to the United States, I realized that I had to change to survive. I used to keep to myself, but now I realize how important it is to have good friends."

Vocabulary
apparently
assess
consist
deviate
document
invest
minimum
strategy
virtual
welfare

Word Study
• The Suffix -*ly*
• Word Forms
• Multiple Meanings

Shemeram is from Iraq.

Vocabulary in Context

Look at the photos and read the text. Respond to the text.

Have you traveled to a faraway place? The first things you notice are appearances, or how things and people look. **Apparently** the people are very different from you. They dress and behave differently. But when you get to know them, you find similarities.

Where would you like to visit?

Before you travel to a place, you should spend time and energy learning about it. When you **invest** in research, you can obtain important information. If you are going to South America, for example, you should know that the Andes Mountains **consist** of miles of high peaks and volcanoes.

Today computers let you take **virtual** journeys. You do not travel in miles. Instead you use technology to "see" new places. This kind of journey requires a **minimum** amount of effort. With very little work, you can see a great deal. You can also do research for a real trip.

What virtual journeys would you take?

Definitions

Read the definitions and example sentences.

apparently (ə-par′-ənt-lē)

adverb seemingly; according to what you can see

Apparently a mouse had been in the kitchen.

consist (kən-sist′)

verb to be formed or made up of

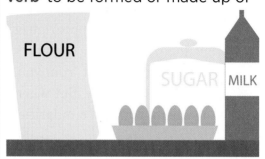

FLOUR

SUGAR MILK

Most cakes **consist** of flour, eggs, milk, and sugar.

invest (in-vest′)

verb to spend money, energy, or time for later benefit

Musicians **invest** time and energy in their playing.

minimum (mi′-nə-məm)

adjective smallest number; least amount

You should eat a **minimum** of three kinds of vegetables a day.

virtual (vər′-chə-wəl)

adjective not real; computer-generated

I took a **virtual** tour of the White House.

Choose one word to draw in this space.

Definitions Check

A Write the word from the box that matches the two examples in each item.

apparently	consist	invest	minimum	virtual

1. _____
to spend many hours studying
to put effort into an art project

2. _____
the fewest people to play a game
the lowest cost for something

3. _____
an online store
a video game

4. _____
to be made up of twelve months
to have seven players

B Write the word from the box that relates to each group of words.

apparently	consist	invest	minimum	virtual

_____ **1.** are, contain, include

_____ **2.** noticeably, clearly

_____ **3.** give, contribute

_____ **4.** computerized, imaginary

_____ **5.** smallest, least, lowest

C Write the word from the box that answers each question.

apparently	consist	invest	minimum	virtual

1. Which word goes with *computer images*? _____

2. Which word goes with *to be made up of*? _____

3. Which word goes with *by what you can see*? _____

4. Which word goes with *to give your energy to*? _____

5. Which word goes with *the least effort*? _____

Students use a computer to take a virtual trip.

A Virtual Vacation

Did you know you can travel to almost any location from the comfort of your home or a local library? To go on a **virtual** trip, all you need is a computer and the Internet, so these safe trips have a **minimum** amount of risk. You can see interesting sights, hear music, and even meet people from around the world. You can take voyages to museums, art galleries, other countries, or even outer space. The destinations are almost limitless!

To begin a virtual trip, you don't have to spend money. Instead, you **invest** your time and energy exploring Web sites about an interesting location. You can quickly find colorful photos and information about diverse lands. You won't be alone as you travel. Teens all over the world are taking virtual trips. **Apparently** they enjoy this kind of travel! Some Web sites even allow teens from different countries to communicate through instant messages and e-mail.

Some travelers keep journals, where they write stories and poems or draw illustrations. In a virtual travel journal, you can copy and paste letters and e-mails you exchange with new friends. Your travel journal can **consist** of everything you want to remember about your virtual trip. What places would you explore on a virtual trip?

Comprehension Check

A Write T if the sentence is true. Write F if the sentence is false.

_____ 1. A trip by computer involves only a **minimum** amount of risk.

_____ 2. A **virtual** trip lets teens see photos of many places.

_____ 3. Virtual travelers do not **invest** any time in their trips.

_____ 4. **Apparently** there are no photos on Web sites.

_____ 5. Virtual trips **consist** mostly of flights on airplanes.

B Write the word from the box that completes each sentence.

apparently	consists	invest	minimal	virtual

What is a (1) _____ trip? It (2) _____

of looking at Web sites that tell about a place. You don't need to

(3) _____ any time in travel, and the planning takes

a (4) _____ amount of effort. Travel Web sites get

many hits. Virtual trips are (5) _____ very popular!

C Write the word or phrase from the box that replaces the underlined words.

apparently	consist	invested	a minimum of	virtual

_____ 1. Today, people can take <u>computer-generated</u> trips.

_____ 2. <u>As I see it</u>, a virtual trip can be as fun as a real trip.

_____ 3. Many travel Web sites <u>are made up</u> of photos and stories about a place.

_____ 4. You should explore <u>at least</u> three Web sites.

_____ 5. You will be happy that you <u>spent</u> your time on this journey.

Word Study The Suffix -ly

A suffix is a part of a word that has a meaning of its own. It comes at the end of a word. A common suffix is -ly. Some words that have this suffix are *apparently, significantly,* and *positively.*

Word	Root	Suffix	Meaning
apparently	*apparent* = clear or easy to see		in a clear way
significantly	*significant* = important; meaningful; major	*ly* = in a certain way	in a meaningful way; in a major way
positively	*positive* = favorable; good		in a good way

1 significantly (*significant* + *ly*)

The word *significant* means "important, meaningful, or major."
Significantly is an adverb that means "in an important, meaningful, or major way."

Coffee and tea are different from each other <u>in an important way</u>.

Jack and his twin brother Jim are different from each other <u>in a big way</u>.

Coffee and tea are **significantly** different from each other.

Jack and his twin brother Jim are **significantly** different from each other.

2 positively (*positive* + *ly*)

The word *positive* means "favorable or good."
Positively is an adverb that means "in a positive way."

Alberta reacted <u>in a positive way</u> to the ending of the movie.

Juan's piano teacher has influenced him <u>in a positive way</u>.

Alberta reacted **positively** to the ending of the movie.

Juan's piano teacher has influenced him **positively**.

Word Study Check The Suffix -*ly*

A **For each word, circle the suffix and underline the root.**

Example: <u>obvious</u>(ly)

1. apparently

2. significantly

3. positively

B **Circle the word that completes each sentence.**

In stores, what is (**apparently, positively**) high quality is not always high

quality. A name-brand purse might not be (**positively, significantly**)

different from a purse without a brand name. By paying attention, people

choose (**positively, apparently**) instead of wasting money.

C **Complete each sentence.**

1. The person who has influenced me the most positively is _____

_____.

2. I know people whose opinions differ significantly about _____

_____.

3. Apparently most students like to _____

_____.

D **Circle the word that has a very different meaning from the other
three words in its row.**

1. clearly   darkly   apparently   obviously

2. positively   happily   favorably   badly

3. lately   notably   meaningfully   significantly

Lesson 13 Wrap-up

 ## Talk About It

Discuss questions 1–5 with a partner.

Topic:
A journey I would like to go on

Details:

1. What would your journey **consist** of?

2. How would you take a **virtual** journey to this place?

3. What is the **minimum** amount of equipment you would need?

4. How much effort would you **invest** in this virtual journey? Why?

5. Why do teens **apparently** enjoy virtual journeys?

Write About It

Write on the lines below about taking a journey. Use ideas from Talk About It.

Topic:
I would like to go on a virtual journey to _____

_____.

Details:

1. My journey would consist of _____

_____.

2. To take a virtual journey to this place, I would ____

_____

_____.

3. The minimum amount of equipment I would

need is _____.

4. The amount of effort I would invest is _____.

because _____

_____.

5. I think teens apparently enjoy virtual journeys

because _____.

Vocabulary in Context

Look at the photos and read the text. Respond to the text.

Apparently some travelers prefer extreme vacations to normal ones. These wild adventures have become more and more popular.

When people plan an extreme journey, they can choose from a range of activities. The journey may **consist** of a climb up a mountain, a jump from an airplane, or a bike trip across a desert. Which of these journeys sounds fun to you?

Before choosing a journey, you should evaluate it based on what you want. You can research different types of adventures to **assess** them based on your needs.

Next, you can make a plan to have the experience you want. Your **strategy** might include joining an extreme vacation club. What is another strategy?

After you make your plan to have an extreme adventure, you should try not to **deviate** from it. You should stick to your plan so that you will really do what you want to do.

An extreme adventure may help you discover your abilities and strengths. What adventure would you choose?

Definitions

Read the definitions and example sentences.

apparently (ə-par′-ənt-lē)

adverb seemingly; according to what you can see

Lata's lunch is still at home. **Apparently** she forgot it.

assess (ə-ses′)

verb to evaluate; to determine the significance of something

City workers **assess** the damage after every storm.

consist (kən-sist′)

verb to be formed or made up of

The gift baskets **consist** of apples, oranges, and bananas.

deviate (dē′-vē-āt′)

verb to turn away from a course or path

The pilot had to **deviate** from her flight plan because of bad weather.

strategy (stra′-tə-jē)

noun a plan of action to accomplish a goal

Li's **strategy** for shopping quickly is to buy only what is on his list.

Choose one word to draw in this space.

Definitions Check

A Match the beginning of each sentence with its ending.

_____ 1. She is apparently unhappy   **a.** from his main message.

_____ 2. The test will assess   **b.** is to ask for advice first.

_____ 3. His lunch will consist of   **c.** the speed of the car.

_____ 4. This speaker did not deviate   **d.** a sandwich, soup, and milk.

_____ 5. My strategy for deciding   **e.** because she is frowning.

B Put a check by the sentence that uses the bold word correctly.

_____ 1. The trees are bending over, so **apparently** a storm is coming.

_____ The willow trees grew **apparently** near the lake.

_____ 2. Jana will **assess** the guitar store through the door in the alley.

_____ Jana will **assess** the guitars based on three criteria.

_____ 3. The final exam will **consist** of a reading passage and an essay.

_____ To make a cake, the baker will **consist** the ingredients together.

_____ 4. She will not **deviate** from her plan to visit China.

_____ Bill will **deviate** until his friends believe him.

_____ 5. According to Elly's class **strategy,** she goes to math after lunch.

_____ Elly's **strategy** for being on time to school is to set two alarms.

C Circle the answer to each question. The answer is in the question. The first one has been done for you.

1. If someone is _apparently_ tired, is she hurrying or (yawning)?

2. Do you _deviate_ from a person or a course?

3. Does your lunch _consist_ of what you eat or where you eat?

4. If you _assess_ an experience, do you evaluate it or forget it?

5. If you use a _strategy,_ do you expect to meet a goal or take a chance?

A tornado chaser took this picture.

Tornado Chasers

Tornado chasers are adventurers, scientists, and filmmakers who follow tornadoes while they are happening. All of these people are taking a big risk. A tornado **consists** of strong winds and a large funnel cloud that touches Earth. A tornado is like a large vacuum because it will suck up almost anything from the ground. What do you see in the photo?

Scientists chase tornadoes in order to collect data and **assess** the causes of these funnel clouds. They also study the tornado's movements. A tornado can quickly switch direction as it travels. Some tornado chasers study why tornadoes suddenly **deviate** from one path to go in a different direction. Scientists want to be able to predict where a tornado will travel. They hope that this knowledge will help city and town officials to create better safety **strategies** for protecting their citizens.

Filmmakers and photographers chase tornadoes to shoot dramatic pictures or videos of these storms. All tornado chasers realize that they may face danger because these powerful storms can cause serious damage to people, animals, and buildings. They can lift a car right into the air. But **apparently** tornado chasers enjoy chasing a storm at the peak of its power.

Why do you think tornado chasers take such big risks?

Comprehension Check

A **Write T if the sentence is true. Write F if the sentence is false.**

_____ 1. People who chase tornadoes **apparently** fear adventure.

_____ 2. Tornadoes **consist** of funnel clouds and strong winds.

_____ 3. A tornado often **deviates** from the path it is on.

_____ 4. Scientists cannot **assess** tornadoes if they follow them.

_____ 5. Town officials like to have **strategies** for tornado safety.

B **Write the word from the box that completes each sentence.**

apparently	assess	consist	deviate	strategies

Tornadoes (1) _____ of powerful winds and

funnel clouds. Tornadoes often (2) _____ from

their paths. Scientists study tornadoes to (3) _____

their causes. Many tornado chasers think their work is exciting, so they

(4) _____ enjoy the adventure. They also want to

help towns make (5) _____ to keep people safe.

C **Write the word from the box that replaces the underlined words.**

apparently	assess	consist	deviate	strategy

_____ 1. Tornado chasers follow tornadoes even when they
<u>turn aside</u> from their paths.

_____ 2. Scientists <u>examine</u> the funnel clouds in a tornado.

_____ 3. Tornadoes <u>are made up</u> of powerful winds and
funnel clouds.

_____ 4. Scientists have a <u>plan</u> for chasing tornadoes safely.

_____ 5. <u>It looks as if</u> tornado chasers enjoy taking risks.

Word Study Word Forms

Words often have several different forms. Read below about some of the different word forms of *consist*.

1 *consistent* (adjective)

A person who is *consistent* acts or thinks the same way most of the time. A thing that is *consistent* does not change or vary.

Jorge's speeches always **consist** of humor as well as facts.

All of his paintings **consist** of red, orange, and yellow designs.

Jorge's speeches are **consistent** because they always include humor as well as facts.

His paintings are **consistent** in their use of red, orange, and yellow.

2 *consistency* (noun)

Consistency is the quality of being the same throughout or all the time. Things can have *consistency*. People can show *consistency*.

The chef makes sure all the pasta dishes **consist** of the same ingredients.

The organization **consists** only of volunteers who are teenagers.

The chef guarantees **consistency** in her pasta dishes.

The organization shows **consistency** in the volunteers it accepts. All the volunteers are teenagers.

Word Study Check Word Forms

A **Circle the word that completes each sentence.**

During the school year, all of Adrie's weekdays (**consist, consistency**) of school, piano lessons, and band. Her weekends are usually much less (**consistent, consistency**). Although she enjoys her weekends, she prefers the (**consist, consistency**) of her weekdays.

B **Complete each sentence.**

1. My weekdays usually consist of _____

_____.

2. One consistent thing in my life is _____

_____.

3. I enjoy having consistency in _____

_____.

C **Match each word to its meaning.**

_____ 1. consist   **a.** the quality of being the same throughout

_____ 2. consistency   **b.** not changing or not varying

_____ 3. consistent   **c.** to be formed or made up of

D **Write the word from the box that completes each sentence.**

consist	consistency	consistent

1. If you always do a thing the same way, then you are _____.

2. Your day may _____ of many different activities.

3. You show _____ by doing your chores every day.

Lesson 14 Wrap-up

 Talk About It

Discuss questions 1–5 with a partner.

Topic:
Planning to take a journey

Details:

1. **Apparently** many people plan their journeys before they go. Why?

2. If you planned a journey, what activities would it **consist** of?

3. What **strategy** would you use to make sure you have a good time?

4. During your journey, why might you need to **deviate** from your plan?

5. How could you **assess** the journey after you returned?

 Write About It

Write about planning a journey on the lines below. Use ideas from Talk About It.

Topic:
Planning a journey is _____

_____.

Details:

1. Apparently many people plan their journeys before

    they leave. This is because _____

    _____.

2. A journey I plan would consist of activities such as _____

    _____.

3. The strategy I would use to make sure I have a good time is

    _____.

4. One reason I might deviate from my plan is _____

    _____.

5. I could assess my journey after I returned by _____

    _____.

Vocabulary in Context

Look at the photos and read the text. Respond to the text.

How would you feel about traveling to Mars? The only way to do this now is to take a **virtual** trip. A computer makes the trip seem real, even though it's not.

Your parents won't be concerned about your **welfare,** because you'll be safe at home. You won't need a passport or any other travel **document.** You won't even need a suitcase!

Before your virtual trip, you should make a plan. Your **strategy** may include using the Internet to find articles about and photographs of Mars. The Mars Exploration Rovers, two robots that have been on Mars since 2003, use cameras to collect images of the planet's surface.

What else might you need for your virtual journey?

After your journey, you may **assess** how it went. Did you learn everything possible about Mars? Do you feel like you've really been there?

What other questions would help you assess the trip?

Definitions

Read the definitions and example sentences.

assess (ə-ses′)

verb to evaluate; to determine the significance of something

Arturo studied the plant to **assess** whether it needed more water.

document (dä′-kyə-mənt′)

noun something written or printed that gives information or proof

The letter from President Lincoln is an important historical **document.**

strategy (stra′-tə-jē)

noun a plan of action to accomplish a goal

Kripa has a **strategy** for getting to the concert.

virtual (vər′-chə-wəl)

adjective not real; computer-generated

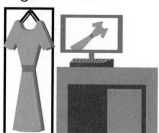

Mrs. Nagle sells dresses through a **virtual** store.

welfare (wel′-fer′)

noun a state of well-being

Mrs. Sevilla worried about the **welfare** of her sick son.

Choose one word to draw in this space.

132

Definitions Check

A **Put a check by the answer to each question.**

1. Which sentence is an example of someone making a document?
   _____ Jorge listened to a recording of his interview with the senator.
   _____ Jorge typed his interview on the computer and then printed it.

2. Which sentence is an example of caring about a person's welfare?
   _____ I asked Ana if she knew who won the baseball game.
   _____ I asked Ana if she had a safe way to get home.

3. Which sentence is an example of how a person might assess something?
   _____ Lakshmi put on her helmet before she rode the bicycle.
   _____ Lakshmi tested the bicycle to make sure it was safe to ride.

4. Which sentence is an example of someone playing a virtual game?
   _____ Lara played a golf game on her computer.
   _____ Lara played a soccer game in the park on Saturday.

B **Write the word from the box that completes each sentence.**

assess	document	strategy	virtual	welfare

1. I have a _____ for making sure I pass my test.

2. A president must protect a nation's _____.

3. She had to _____ many options and choose one.

4. Marina read the _____ before she signed it.

5. Student pilots practice flying _____ airplanes.

C **Complete the sentences below.**

1. A document I have created is _____.

2. A doctor may assess _____.

3. I worry about the welfare of _____.

4. My strategy for being on time to school is _____.

5. People shop at virtual stores because _____.

This person types without using her hands.

Everyday Journeys with Technology

Most people travel every day with ease, but for some people with disabilities, even a short journey can present obstacles. For a person in a wheelchair, getting onto a bus or climbing a building's stairs can be difficult. The person must **assess** these challenges and ask, "How can I overcome this?" What other obstacles do people with disabilities face?

People find **strategies** for overcoming these challenges. Technology can help. Elevators carry visitors to buildings' upper floors, and many buses now have special lifts for people who cannot climb the steps. This technology improves conditions for people with disabilities.

Technology improves the **welfare** of people with disabilities in other ways, too. People who cannot use their hands use a technology called "voice recognition software" to operate computers. A person uses his or her voice, instead of a keyboard or a mouse, to tell a computer what to do. This technology allows people to create **documents** without using their hands to type. People can also use this technology to browse the Internet. They can shop at **virtual** stores, read news articles, and visit all sorts of other Web sites.

Everyone can use assistance. What technologies assist you?

Comprehension Check

A **Write T if the sentence is true. Write F if the sentence is false.**

_____ 1. Voice recognition software helps people create **documents**.

_____ 2. People can create **strategies** for overcoming obstacles.

_____ 3. You must climb stairs to reach a **virtual** store.

_____ 4. People can **assess** the difficulties they face on a journey.

_____ 5. Technology has done little to improve the **welfare** of people with disabilities.

B **Write the word from the box that completes each sentence.**

assess	documents	strategies	virtual	welfare

People with disabilities must (1) _____ obstacles

and develop (2) _____ to overcome them.

Technology can help, and it improves the (3) _____

of many people with disabilities. People use technology to type

(4) _____ without their hands. They also use it

to visit (5) _____ stores and other Web sites.

C **Write the word from the box that replaces the underlined words.**

assess	document	strategies	virtual	welfare

_____ 1. Technology contributes to people's <u>well-being</u>.

_____ 2. People form <u>plans of action</u> for overcoming obstacles.

_____ 3. Many people shop at <u>computer-generated</u> stores.

_____ 4. One way to create a <u>piece of written information</u> is by typing it.

_____ 5. How can you <u>figure out</u> the value of technology?

Word Study Multiple Meanings

A word often has more than one meaning. Read about two different meanings of *document*.

1 *document:* (noun) something written or printed that gives information or proof

- a handwritten **document**
- a **document** that proves your age
- an electronic **document**
- a historical **document**

Allison looked at an important **document** at the historical society.

An e-mail is a type of electronic **document**.

2 *document:* (verb) to prove or support with written or printed information

- to **document** a conversation
- to **document** history
- to **document** a case in court
- to **document** a crime

Susan must **document** all of her interviews by taking notes.

If your bicycle is stolen, you should **document** what happened by filing a police report.

Word Study Check Multiple Meanings

A For each numbered item, choose *a* or *b* as the correct meaning of the word in bold.

document
a. (noun) something written or printed that gives information or proof
b. (verb) to prove or support with written or printed information

1. _____ My teacher asked me to **document** my research.

2. _____ The officer asked for a **document** that shows my name and address.

3. _____ Ray created a **document** on his computer.

4. _____ The phone company will **document** our phone calls.

B Write "Yes" or "No" to answer each question.

_____ 1. Can you document a court case?

_____ 2. Is a telephone conversation a document?

_____ 3. Is it possible to document a conversation?

_____ 4. Can you document a story about a historical person?

_____ 5. Can a document prove your date of birth?

_____ 6. Is a fact you hear on television a document?

C Follow the directions below. Write your answers on the lines.

1. List two things that are **documents**.

   _____

   _____

2. List two things that you can **document**.

   _____

   _____

Lesson 15 Wrap-up

 Talk About It

Discuss questions 1–5 with a partner.

Topic:
Taking your own virtual journey

Details:

1. How can you take a **virtual** journey?

2. What would your **strategy** be for this journey?

3. Will people worry about your **welfare**? Why or why not?

4. How can you **assess** the information you find about your destination?

5. What **documents** might you use or create during your virtual trip?

Write About It

Write about a virtual journey on the lines below. Use ideas from Talk About It.

Topic:

I would take a virtual journey to _____.

Details:

1. I can take a virtual journey by _____

   _____.

2. My strategy for taking this virtual journey

   would be _____

   _____.

3. People will not worry about my welfare because

   _____.

4. I can assess the information I find about my destination

   by _____.

5. Documents I might use on my trip are _____

   _____. Documents I might create during my

   trip are _____.

Unit 5 Wrap-up

 Think About It

Think about the words you learned in Unit 5. Have you mastered them? Write each word under the right heading: Words I Have Mastered or Words I Need to Review. Make sentences using the words to prepare for the Unit Assessment.

Vocabulary Words

apparently	invest
assess	minimum
consist	strategy
deviate	virtual
document	welfare

Words I Have Mastered

_____   _____

_____   _____

_____   _____

_____   _____

_____   _____

Words I Need to Review

_____   _____

_____   _____

_____   _____

Practice Sentences

_____

_____

_____

_____

_____

_____

_____

_____

Unit 5 Assessment

A Read the entries in this travel journal.

Circle the word that completes each sentence.

May 25

I am in Mexico City. Tomorrow I plan to visit the Palace of
Fine Arts. Today I took a (**minimum, virtual**) tour of it on the
computer. The building is made of white marble. (**Strategy,
Apparently**), the government decided it was a good idea to
(**assess, invest**) in strong, beautiful materials. And the art inside
the museum is too valuable to (**assess, consist**). My (**strategy,
document**) for seeing everything is to start with the murals by
Diego Rivera and go from there.

Write a word from the box to complete each sentence.

consists	deviate	documents	minimum	welfare

May 26

The Palace of Fine Arts is a beautiful place! Inside the
museum, I read some (1) _____ that told its
story. But I didn't want to (2) _____ too
far from my plan of seeing the murals. I knew it would take a
(3) _____ of two hours to see them all. The
museum (4) _____ of an amazing variety of
artifacts and works of art. The museum staff works hard to
protect the (5) _____ of each piece.

B Circle the letter of the answer that best completes each sentence.

1. An apple is _____ larger than a grape.
   a. significantly
   b. mutually
   c. flexibly

2. She has a _____ record of winning.
   a. consists
   b. consistent
   c. consistency

3. The _____ that I sent contains important information.
   a. strategy
   b. document
   c. welfare

4. I plan to _____ all cases of bullying.
   a. document
   b. deviate
   c. consist

C Circle the letter of the answer that means the same thing as the underlined word or phrase.

1. He responded <u>positively</u> to my letter.
   a. in a quiet way
   b. in a rude way
   c. in a good way

2. When I travel, I like to <u>document</u> everything I see.
   a. enjoy
   b. try a little of
   c. keep a record of

3. The builder wants <u>consistency</u> among all the houses he builds.
   a. strategy
   b. similarity
   c. apparently

4. <u>Apparently</u> she does not like the meal.
   a. It seems that
   b. I doubt that
   c. Significantly

D For each item, write a sentence that uses both words.

1. apparently, minimum

_____

_____

2. consist, virtual

_____

_____

3. deviate, strategy

_____

_____

How Does Nature Touch Lives?

"Back in Ponce, I saw green trees, brown mountains, blue oceans, white beaches, and lots of other natural color. I miss all the colors."

Joan is from Puerto Rico.

Vocabulary in Context

Look at the photos and read the text. Respond to the text.

What makes a Mexican shrimp plant unusual? Its leaves look like shrimp! If you grow this unusual plant indoors, make sure it gets enough sunlight. You can **maximize** the sunlight it receives by keeping it near a window. Just make sure the plant is not in direct sunlight.

You can also grow shrimp plants outdoors. If your family has a yard, you can ask them to help you change part of it into a garden. If they agree to **convert** a portion of your yard, choose a spot partially in the shade for the shrimp plants. If a shrimp plant gets too much direct sunlight, it is **inevitable** that it will wilt.

Before you buy any plant, make sure you have the time and the knowledge to properly care for it. It takes **considerable** effort to become a successful gardener.

Why will you be more likely to **persist** in this effort if you do research first?

Definitions

Read the definitions and example sentences.

considerable (kən-si'-dər-ə-bəl)

adjective significant; worthy of notice

Graduating from high school is a **considerable** achievement.

convert (kən-vərt')

verb to change something into something else

BANCO

You need to **convert** dollars into pesos when you travel to Mexico.

inevitable (i-ne'-və-tə-bəl)

adjective sure to happen

When the sky is gray and cloudy, rain is almost **inevitable.**

maximize (mak'-sə-mīz')

verb to increase as much as possible

We moved the table to **maximize** the size of the dance floor.

persist (pər-sist')

verb to refuse to stop or give up; to remain in existence

The race is long, but Jae will **persist** until he reaches the finish line.

Choose one word to draw in this space.

Definitions Check

A
Write the word from the box that matches the two examples in each item.

considerable	convert	inevitable	maximize	persist

1. _____
to change water power into electricity
to change a sofa into a bed

2. _____
to strive to reach an important goal
to keep running even if you are tired

3. _____
the sun rising and setting each day
growing older

4. _____
to make the most of study time
to increase the width of a street

B
Write the word from the box that relates to each group of words.

considerable	convert	inevitable	maximize	persist

_____ **1.** expected, definite, predictable

_____ **2.** continue, sustain, try

_____ **3.** important, meaningful, major

_____ **4.** switch, change, exchange

_____ **5.** enlarge, biggest, increase

C
Write the word from the box that answers each question.

considerable	convert	inevitable	maximize	persist

1. Which word goes with *you can't escape it*? _____

2. Which word goes with *a big deal*? _____

3. Which word goes with *don't give up*? _____

4. Which word goes with *get the most out of*? _____

5. Which word goes with *change to another religion*? _____

A Venus flytrap captures an insect.

Venus Flytraps

Carnivorous plants are plants that can eat meat! These plants live in environments where they can't get enough nutrients from the soil alone. These plants **persist** in their environments by eating insects. Sometimes they even eat frogs and other small animals.

The Venus flytrap is a carnivorous plant that grows in the southwestern United States. Venus flytraps **maximize** their chances of survival by eating insects. Trapping an insect is a **considerable** accomplishment for a plant! Have you ever seen a Venus flytrap eat a fly? If so, describe what you saw.

Tiny hairs cover the leaves of a Venus flytrap. When an insect touches these hairs, the leaves snap closed. The leaves then take in nutrients from the insect. The nutrients help the plant to **convert** sunlight into energy.

Venus flytraps are easier to grow than most carnivorous plants. Consequently, Venus flytraps are popular houseplants. Although you can find Venus flytraps in plant stores, they are becoming less common in the wild. It is **inevitable** that Venus flytraps will become extinct in their natural environments unless people work to protect them.

What could people do to help protect the Venus flytrap?

Comprehension Check

A Write T if the sentence is true. Write F if the sentence is false.

_____ 1. Venus flytraps must **maximize** their chances of dying.

_____ 2. Some plants **persist** in their environments by eating flies.

_____ 3. Venus flytraps **convert** flies into frogs.

_____ 4. For some wild plants, extinction is almost **inevitable**.

_____ 5. Eating an insect is a **considerable** accomplishment for a plant.

B Write the word from the box that completes each sentence.

considerable	convert	inevitable	maximize	persist

Venus flytraps achieve a (1) _____ feat. They

(2) _____ their nutrients by catching insects. The

insides of insects help these plants to (3) _____

sunlight into energy. Venus flytraps can (4) _____ in

their environments as a result. The extinction of the Venus flytrap does not

have to be (5) _____.

C Write the word from the box that replaces the underlined words.

considerable	convert	inevitable	maximize	persisted

_____ 1. For many years the committee <u>refused to give up</u> in the fight to save natural land.

_____ 2. Living things work to <u>increase</u> their chance of survival.

_____ 3. Extinction is <u>certain</u> for many types of plants.

_____ 4. People can be a <u>significant</u> help to plants in the wild.

_____ 5. Most plants <u>change</u> water and sunlight into energy.

Word Study Word Forms

Words often have several different forms. Read below about some of the different forms of *persist.*

1 *persistent* (adjective)

If someone is *persistent,* he or she tries again and again without giving up.

Mateo **persisted** in trying to sell me the candy.

When Dee's cold **persisted,** she called the doctor.

Mateo was **persistent** in trying to sell me the candy.

Dee's cold was so **persistent** that she called the doctor.

2 *persistence* (noun)

Persistence is the act of trying again and again without giving up.

It is important to be **persistent** in the search for a job.

He was quite bothered when the fly **persisted** in jumping on and off his forehead.

Persistence is important in the search for a job.

He was quite bothered by the **persistence** of the fly, which jumped on and off his forehead.

Word Study Check Word Forms

A **Circle the word that completes each sentence.**

Jamila (**persisted, persistence**) in her effort to become class president. She

is a very (**persist, persistent**) person. Her (**persistence, persistent**) helped

her reach her goal.

B **Complete each sentence.**

1. A persistent person is someone who _____

_____.

2. I proved my persistence when I _____

_____.

3. This week I persisted in _____

_____.

C **Match each word to its meaning.**

_____ 1. persist   **a.** not likely to give up

_____ 2. persistence   **b.** the act or quality of not giving up

_____ 3. persistent   **c.** to try again and again without giving up

D **Write the word from the box that completes each sentence.**

persist	persistence	persistent

1. A _____ actor keeps trying until he gets a part
   in a play.

2. Manuela will _____ in her goal of becoming
   an engineer.

3. Your _____ will help you reach your goal.

Lesson 16 Wrap-up

 ## Talk About It

Discuss questions 1–5 with a partner.

Topic:
Protecting unusual things in nature

Details:

1. Why are differences in plants and animals **inevitable**?

2. What kinds of living things can **convert** from one form to another?

3. Why is the Venus flytrap in **considerable** danger?

4. How can people **maximize** their awareness of environmental issues?

5. Why should people **persist** in an effort to protect all living things?

Write About It

Write about protecting unusual things in nature on the lines below. Use ideas from Talk About It.

Topic:
It is important to protect unusual things in nature because _____

_____.

Details:

1. Differences in plants and animals are inevitable because

_____.

2. Some living things can convert from one form to

another, such as _____.

3. The Venus flytrap, a plant that eats insects, is in

considerable danger because _____.

_____.

4. People can maximize their awareness of environmental

issues by _____.

5. People should persist in an effort to protect living things

because _____.

Vocabulary in Context

Look at the photos and read the text. Respond to the text.

The idea of eating raw fish is new to many Americans. But this **concept** is not new around the world. A **considerable** number of people eat raw fish as part of their diet.

Do you like raw fish? If you have not tried it, would you like to?

Sushi is a type of food that often includes raw fish. It comes from Japan. Recently sushi has become a lot more popular in the United States. Some people connect this change to the growth of international communities. They **attribute** it to the mixing of cultures.

How many restaurants in your area serve sushi?

People have **conceived** many ways of preparing raw fish. In Scandinavia, lutefisk is prepared with a solution called lye. In Latin America, raw fish is "cooked" with lemon juice to make ceviche. These foods have been around for many years. They **persist** in people's diets today. In your family's country, how is fish prepared?

Definitions

Read the definitions and example sentences.

attribute (ə-triˈ-būtˈ)

verb to think of as caused by

I **attribute** my musical talent to my father.

conceive (kən-sēvˈ)

verb to form or develop in the mind

Joan could not **conceive** of eating grasshoppers.

concept (känˈ-septˈ)

noun a general idea or thought

Ms. Taylor teaches the **concept** of sharing in her class.

considerable (kən-siˈ-dər-ə-bəl)

adjective significant; worthy of notice

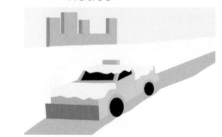

New York City gets a **considerable** amount of snow each year.

persist (pər-sistˈ)

verb to refuse to stop or give up; to remain in existence

This is Bob's fifth call, but he will **persist** until he gets a date.

Choose one word to draw in this space.

Definitions Check

A Match the beginning of each sentence with its ending.

_____ 1. Free speech is

_____ 2. They attribute their success

_____ 3. The cold weather will persist

_____ 4. She has a considerable

_____ 5. He cannot conceive of

a. to their hard work.

b. dinner without dessert.

c. talent for music.

d. an important concept.

e. until April or May.

B Put a check by the sentence that uses the bold word correctly.

_____ 1. The director needed a new **concept** for a TV show.

_____   Jamal had the **concept** to go out for dinner tonight.

_____ 2. Raúl will **persist** in practicing the drums until he plays well.

_____   Mr. Repp will **persist** his students to learn World History.

_____ 3. Jan was **considerable** when he tutored a younger student.

_____   He spends a **considerable** amount of time reading magazines.

_____ 4. I **attribute** the pain in my back to the gardening I did yesterday.

_____   I **attribute** money to the garden club every year.

_____ 5. He always tells the truth, so he will never **conceive** anyone.

_____   He cannot **conceive** of lying to anyone.

C Circle the answer to each question. The answer is in the question. The first one has been done for you.

1. Do you _conceive_ (ideas) or shoes?

2. Is a _considerable_ effort very big or very small?

3. If you _persist_ in a job, do you give up or work hard?

4. Would you _attribute_ a flood to a rainstorm or a heat wave?

5. Is a _concept_ an idea or a challenge?

The giant barb is one kind of large freshwater fish.

The Megafishes Project

Can you imagine catching a fish that weighs one thousand pounds? Can you imagine trying to save it? In 2004 Dr. Zeb Hogan thought of the **concept** of protecting giant freshwater fish. The idea he **conceived** led to the Megafishes Project. The project is the first worldwide attempt to help save these large freshwater fish. This project requires a **considerable** amount of effort. People document and study giant fish in more than seventeen different countries, including the United States and China.

Scientists on the Megafishes Project study why these large fish are disappearing. They have **attributed** the disappearance of the fish to the overuse of fresh water. What are ways that people overuse water?

Dr. Hogan conceived the idea of finding the largest freshwater fish. Two of the large fish that his team identified are the giant Chinese sturgeon and the Chinese paddlefish. The paddlefish may be the world's largest freshwater fish. It can grow to be 23 feet long and can weigh up to 1,100 pounds! Hogan and his team **persist** in their efforts to identify and protect these large fish. What other large fish have you heard about?

Comprehension Check

A   Write T if the sentence is true. Write F if the sentence is false.

_____ **1.** A **considerable** number of fish are in danger of extinction.

_____ **2.** Scientists **attribute** this danger to the overuse of freshwater.

_____ **3.** Scientists **persist** in their search for large fish.

_____ **4.** Scientists believe the **concept** that large fish are in only one country.

_____ **5.** Scientists **conceived** a project to study very small fish.

B   Write the word from the box that completes each sentence.

attribute	conceived	concept	considerable	persist

A (1) _____ number of fish are in danger.

Scientists (2) _____ this to the overuse of water.

A scientist (3) _____ a project to study these

fish. His (4) _____ is that the largest fish must be

identified. Scientists believe it is important to (5) _____

in their search.

C   Write the word from the box that replaces the underlined words.

attribute	conceived	concept	considerable	persist

_____ **1.** The number of freshwater fish in danger is <u>significant</u>.

_____ **2.** Scientists <u>developed</u> a project to save the fish.

_____ **3.** The <u>idea</u> is that the project will identify large fish.

_____ **4.** Scientists must <u>continue</u> in order to succeed.

_____ **5.** Scientists <u>trace</u> the danger that freshwater fish are in to the overuse of freshwater.

Word Study The Root *tribu*

The root of a word is the part that tells us the basic meaning of the word. The root *tribu* comes from the Latin verb *tribuere,* which means "to pay, assign, give out, or grant." Some words that are built from this root are *attribute, contribute,* and *tribute.* You can use the root as a clue to help you understand the meaning of the whole word.

Word	Prefix	Root	Meaning
attribute	*at-* = to, toward, at	*tribu* = to pay, assign, give out, or grant	to assign an effect to a cause
contribute	*con-* = together, with		to give, often together with others
tribute			something given to show thanks or respect

1 contribute (con + tribute)

The prefix *con-* means "together" or "with."
Contribute is a verb that means "to give, often together with others."

We will <u>give</u> money <u>together with others</u> to the school fundraiser.

Stefan likes to <u>give</u> his ideas in discussions <u>with others</u>.

We will **contribute** money to the school fundraiser.

Stefan likes to **contribute** his ideas in discussions.

2 tribute (tribute)

Tribute is a noun that means "something given to show thanks or respect."

The statue is a <u>way to pay respect</u> to soldiers from World War II.

The Mother's Day lunch was a <u>show of thanks</u> to the students' mothers.

The statue is a **tribute** to soldiers from World War II.

The Mother's Day lunch was a **tribute** to the students' mothers.

Word Study Check The Root *tribu*

A For each word, circle the root.

Example: at(tribu)tion

1. attribute

2. contribute

3. tribute

B Circle the word that completes each sentence.

The new sculpture is a (**contribute, tribute**) to the state bird. The bird is

in danger of extinction. Scientists (**attribute, tribute**) the bird's decreasing

population to the removal of trees. People can help if they (**attribute,**

contribute) to the fund to save the state bird.

C Complete each sentence.

1. I attribute my height to _____

_____.

2. To help others, I can contribute to _____

_____.

3. Someday I will give a tribute. The purpose of it will be _____

_____.

D Circle the word that has a very different meaning from the other three
words in its row.

1. tribute   honor   fee   thanks

2. attribute   explain   assign   take

3. leave   contribute   offer   give

Lesson 17 Wrap-up

 Talk About It

Discuss questions 1–5 with a partner.

Topic:
Plants or animals in nature that I would help

Details:

1. What animal in **considerable** danger do you care about?

2. To what do you **attribute** the danger that this animal or plant is in?

3. Will the danger to this animal **persist**?

4. How have our **concepts** about the importance of animals changed?

5. If you had to **conceive** a plan to help your plant or animal, what would it be?

 Write About It

Write about a plant or animal on the lines below. Use ideas from Talk About It.

Topic:
A living thing that I would help is _____.

Details:

1. It is in considerable danger because _____
   _____.

2. I attribute this dangerous condition to _____
   _____.

3. People can persist in their efforts to protect
   living things by _____.

4. Our concepts about the value of living
   things have changed because _____
   _____.

5. If I had to conceive a new way to protect an animal,
   I would first _____.

Vocabulary in Context

Look at the photos and read the text. Respond to the text.

Do you like the idea of tracking and predicting the weather? If this **concept** interests you, you might want to study meteorology, the science of weather.

Someone who wants to practice meteorology as a profession must first get a degree. Only then can he or she be a meteorology **practitioner**. What would it be like to have a job as a meteorologist?

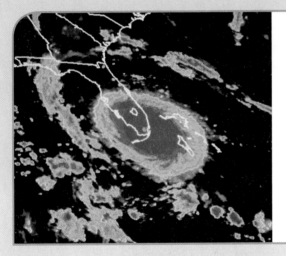

Weather predictions must be very accurate. Meteorologists **maximize** the accuracy of their predictions by looking at past weather patterns. They also update their predictions when they get new information. Meteorologists often must interpret data.

What data do you think meteorologists interpret?

There are different systems of ideas about severe weather. One **philosophy** is that severe weather, such as extreme heat, is caused by global warming. Another philosophy does not **attribute** these weather patterns to global warming. Not all meteorologists follow the same philosophy.

How do you think this affects their predictions?

Definitions

Read the definitions and example sentences.

attribute (ə-tri′-būt′)

verb to think of as caused by

They **attribute** their good health to daily exercise.

concept (kän′-sept′)

noun a general idea or thought

The teacher explained the complex **concept** to the class.

maximize (mak′-sə-mīz′)

verb to increase as much as possible

The tall windows **maximize** the amount of light in the room.

philosophy (fə-lä′-sə-fē)

noun a system of ideas and beliefs

In class we studied the **philosophy** of the ancient Greeks.

practitioner (prak-ti′-shə-nər)

noun a person who works in a trade, field, or profession

A doctor is just one kind of medical **practitioner.**

Choose one word to draw in this space.

Definitions Check

A Put a check by the answer to each question.

1. Which sentence is an example of someone who is a practitioner?
   _____ The nurse helps patients every day.
   _____ Luis is taking his first nursing class.

2. Which sentence is an example of a philosophy?
   _____ It is fun to go to the store on Saturday to shop for food.
   _____ The health of the global community should come before profits.

3. Which sentence is an example of how you maximize something?
   _____ You blow up the balloon until it is almost ready to pop.
   _____ You choose five balloons and blow them up one at a time.

4. Which sentence is an example of someone who has a concept?
   _____ She thinks she can earn money by recycling paper.
   _____ She reads the entire newspaper every day.

B Write the word from the box that completes each sentence.

attribute	concept	maximize	philosophy	practitioner

1. The medical _____ works at the hospital.

2. I _____ the lack of attendance to the snowstorm.

3. Jan is interested in studying Hindu _____.

4. Ly wants to _____ how much weight he can lift.

5. Tula loves the _____ of a bicycle that folds up.

C Complete the sentences below.

1. One kind of dental practitioner is _____.

2. I attribute my success in school to _____.

3. To maximize the space in my room, I could _____.

4. I would like to study the philosophy of _____.

5. A concept I studied in class is _____.

Two weather spotters track temperatures.

Tracking Severe Weather

The National Weather Service (NWS) is in charge of warning people about severe weather. In the 1970s, the NWS conceived the **concept** of a network of volunteers across the country who could report severe weather. They developed this concept into the Skywarn™ program. How do you think this program works?

The NWS's **philosophy** is that weather predictions must be as precise as possible. The Skywarn program helps in two ways. First, volunteers are trained to become **practitioners** of "weather spotting." This means they look for signs of severe weather. Weather spotters may record data about snowfalls, watch rivers that seem ready to flood, or watch the sky for signs that a tornado is forming. Spotters report this data to the NWS. This data **maximizes** the NWS's ability to predict severe weather.

Second, weather spotters check the accuracy of the NWS's weather predictions. They compare the predictions to the actual weather. Some volunteers monitor local climates by measuring temperature and rainfall every day. People are better informed about severe weather than they used to be, and the NWS **attributes** this improvement in part to the Skywarn program.

Would you like being a weather spotter? Explain.

Comprehension Check

A   Write T if the sentence is true. Write F if the sentence is false.

_____ 1. The NWS trains people to be weather-spotting **practitioners**.

_____ 2. The **concept** of using regular people as weather spotters failed.

_____ 3. The NWS and weather spotters have different **philosophies**.

_____ 4. Volunteers help the NWS **maximize** its ability to predict storms.

_____ 5. The NWS **attributes** severe weather to the Skywarn program.

B   Write the word from the box that completes each sentence.

attributes	concept	maximize	philosophy	practitioners

The NWS's (1) _____ is that weather predictions should be precise. They thought of the (2) _____ of having volunteers report weather data. Weather spotters train to be skilled (3) _____. They help (4) _____ the accuracy of storm predictions. The NWS (5) _____ some of its effectiveness to the spotters.

C   Write the word from the box that replaces the underlined words.

attributes	concept	maximize	philosophy	practitioners

_____ 1. The NWS has a <u>system of ideas</u> about forecasting.

_____ 2. The NWS <u>gives credit for</u> people's awareness of severe weather to the Skywarn system.

_____ 3. Meteorologists wanted to <u>increase</u> their ability to warn people about bad weather.

_____ 4. What new <u>idea</u> did the NWS conceive in the 1970s?

_____ 5. Meteorologists are <u>workers in the field</u> of weather forecasting.

Word Study   Word Forms

Words often have several different forms. Read below about some of the different word forms of *concept.*

1 *conception* (noun)

A *conception* is a person's understanding of a thing or idea.

Celia's understanding of the concept of hard work is that it should make you sweat.

Our understanding of the concept of community service is similar.

Celia's **conception** of hard work is that it should make you sweat.

Our **conception** of community service is similar.

2 *conceptualize* (verb)

When you *conceptualize* something, you form thoughts or ideas related to it.

I can form a concept of how electricity works when I complete a simple circuit.

The concept of global warming is difficult for me to picture in my mind.

I can **conceptualize** how electricity works when I create a simple circuit.

It is difficult for me to **conceptualize** the process of global warming.

Word Study Check Word Forms

A **Circle the word that completes each sentence.**

Juan likes the (**concept, conceptualize**) of exercise. His (**concepts, conception**) of a good workout is a long run. Juan is working with other students to (**conceptualize, conception**) a plan to promote physical activity that is fun.

B **Complete each sentence.**

1. I believe in the concept of _____

_____.

2. It is difficult for me to conceptualize _____

_____.

3. My conception of global warming is that _____

_____.

C **Match each word to its meaning.**

_____ 1. conceptualize   **a.** to form thoughts or ideas about

_____ 2. concept   **b.** an understanding of a thing or idea

_____ 3. conception   **c.** a general idea or thought

D **Write the word from the box that completes each sentence.**

concepts	conception	conceptualize

1. In algebra class, you study math _____.

2. I can help you _____ how a car engine works.

3. Not everyone has the same _____ of what makes a movie good.

Lesson 18 Wrap-up

 Talk About It

Discuss questions 1–5 with a partner.

Topic:
The effect of weather on my life

Details:

1. What is your **philosophy** about dealing with difficult weather?

2. How are weather **practitioners** in your home country different from practitioners here?

3. What new **concept** have you recently learned about weather?

4. How do you **maximize** your time outdoors when the weather is nice?

5. When have you **attributed** a bad experience to weather?

 Write About It

Write about how weather affects your life on the lines below. Use ideas from Talk About It.

Topic:
Weather affects my life every day because _____

_____.

Details:

1. My philosophy about dealing with difficult weather

   is that _____.

2. Weather practitioners in my home country are different

   in that they _____.

3. One new weather-related concept that I have learned

   is _____.

4. When the weather is nice, I maximize my time

   outdoors by _____.

5. A bad experience I attributed to the weather was

   _____.

Unit 6 Wrap-up

 Think About It

Think about the words you learned in Unit 6. Have you mastered them? Write each word under the right heading: Words I Have Mastered or Words I Need to Review. Make sentences using the words to prepare for the Unit Assessment.

Words I Have Mastered

_____   _____

_____   _____

_____   _____

_____   _____

Words I Need to Review

_____   _____

_____   _____

_____   _____

Practice Sentences

_____

_____

_____

_____

_____

_____

_____

_____

Unit 6 Assessment

A Read the postcards sent between Joan and Anita.

Circle the word that completes each sentence.

Greetings, Anita!

I'm on a volunteer trip in Lima, Peru, helping people after the earthquake. We want to (**maximize, convert**) the use of our time here. Some of us help (**convert, persist**) damaged buildings into new homes. A medical (**attribute, practitioner**) provides treatment for people. My group shares the same (**practioner, philosophy**). We think it's important to (**persist, convert**) in helping others.

See you soon,
Joan

Anita
123 East Street
Anita's City,
Anita's State
45678
USA

Write a word from the box to complete each sentence.

attribute	conceive	concept	considerable	inevitable

Dear Joan,

The damage from a major earthquake is terrible! It is

(1) _____ that people will suffer. Your group

must be doing a (2) _____ amount of work

to help the victims. How did you (3) _____

of the idea of volunteering in South America? What a great

(4) _____! I will volunteer in my community.

I (5) _____ my interest in volunteering to your

work in Peru.

Joan
c/o Lima
Volunteers
Lima
Peru

Your friend, Anita

168

B Circle the letter of the answer that best completes each sentence.

1. Readers may _____ letters to the newspaper.
   a. tribute
   b. contribute
   c. contribution

2. This show is a _____ to civil rights leaders.
   a. concept
   b. tribute
   c. persistence

3. The _____ athlete does not stop easily.
   a. persistence
   b. persist
   c. persistent

4. Pictures often help people _____ the past.
   a. conceptualize
   b. concept
   c. conception

C Circle the letter of the answer that means the same thing as the underlined word or phrase.

1. She is <u>persistent in</u> her goal to become a geologist.
   a. letting go of
   b. not giving up on
   c. conceptualizing

2. Her <u>persistence</u> impressed us all.
   a. continual effort
   b. weak effort
   c. first effort

3. The singer's performance was <u>a tribute to</u> Frank Sinatra.
   a. a newspaper about
   b. an event to dance with
   c. an event to honor

4. We will <u>contribute</u> clothes to the shelter.
   a. sew
   b. receive
   c. give

D For each item, write a sentence that uses both words.

1. convert, maximize

   _____

   _____

2. attribute, philosophy

   _____

   _____

3. persist, practitioner

   _____

   _____

How Do I Measure Success?

Vocabulary
advocate
component
incentive
modify
monitor
policy
priority
radical
refine
statistics

Word Study
- Multiple Meanings
- Collocations
- The Root *voc*

"I know I have been successful when I see myself achieving something in my mind, and then I make it real."

Chinazor is from Nigeria.

Vocabulary in Context

Look at the photos and read the text. Respond to the text.

How popular do you think museums are? **Statistics** show that 2.3 million people visit American museums every day. For many museums, it is important to teach visitors how people in a different cultures lived, dressed, and survived throughout history. Preserving the culture of these groups is the **priority** for these museums.

Museums are not just about the past. They have to stay up to date on the latest information. For example, museums that focus on Native American culture **monitor** the research of archaeologists who dig at the sites of old Native American settlements. These museums keep track of this research and use it to update their displays.

New discoveries can result in different kinds of changes inside a museum. Museums may **modify** their exhibits in simple ways. For example, they may rewrite new facts on a sign. But some discoveries can cause a **radical** change in an exhibit. The museum may redesign it entirely. What museums have you visited?

Definitions

Read the definitions and example sentences.

modify (mä'-də-fī')

verb to change or alter in some way

Aida will **modify** her robot by adding new wheels.

monitor (mä'-nə-tər)

verb to keep watch over something or someone

Each day I **monitor** how much my new puppy eats.

priority (prī-ôr'-ə-tē)

noun something that ranks high in importance

Ricardo makes homework a **priority** over sports.

radical (ra'-di-kəl)

adjective far from the usual; extreme

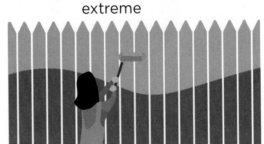

The bright orange color was a **radical** change from brown.

statistics (stə-tis'-tiks)

noun information gathered in the form of numbers

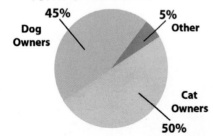

Statistics show that more people in my class have cats than dogs.

Choose one word to draw in this space.

172

Definitions Check

A Write the word from the box that matches the two examples in each item.

modify	monitor	priority	radical	statistics

1. _____
to observe a science experiment
to make sure players follow the rules

2. _____
the main thing you have to do today
the first task on a list

3. _____
the population of a town
the number of students in college

4. _____
an extreme change in the weather
a new plan that is very different

B Write the word from the box that relates to each group of words.

modify	monitor	priority	radical	statistics

_____ 1. change, adapt, edit

_____ 2. first, important, significant

_____ 3. watch, observe, oversee

_____ 4. numbers, data

_____ 5. different, crazy, severe

C Write the word from the box that answers each question.

modify	monitor	priority	radical	statistics

1. Which word goes with *to watch what you eat*? _____

2. Which word goes with *to correct a spelling mistake*? _____

3. Which word goes with *to dye your hair a wild color*? _____

4. Which word goes with *your goal for the year*? _____

5. Which word goes with *how many kids go to school*? _____

People visit a cultural museum.

Museum Honors Arab Americans

Statistics show that the United States has more than 15,000 museums. Some museums make it a priority to focus on one group of people. The Arab American National Museum in Dearborn, Michigan, does just that. It honors Arab Americans, their stories, and their lives.

In one exhibit, visitors learn about Lebanese American George Doumani and his five trips to Antarctica. He was a geologist who helped prove the radical theory of "continental drift." His work proved that Earth's continents are moving and changing shape at a very slow speed.

Another exhibit shows the typewriter of the famous journalist Helen Thomas. This Lebanese American monitored the news at the White House for 57 years! Thomas is known as the "first lady of the press."

In another part of the museum, visitors listen to a recording of a speech by President John F. Kennedy. In it he says the words, "Ask not what your country can do for you—ask what you can do for your country." This idea came from Kahlil Gibran, a Lebanese writer who lived for many years in the United States. The president modified the writer's idea and used it in a major speech. Do you live close enough to Dearborn, Michigan to go to the Arab American National Museum?

Comprehension Check

A **Write T if the sentence is true. Write F if the sentence is false.**

_____ 1. **Statistics** show there are more than 250,000 museums in the United States.

_____ 2. George Doumani proved a **radical** idea in science.

_____ 3. One museum makes it a **priority** to focus on Arab Americans.

_____ 4. President Bush used a **modified** idea from Kahlil Gibran's writings.

_____ 5. Kahlil Gibran **monitored** the news for 57 years.

B **Write the word from the box that completes each sentence.**

modified	monitored	priority	radical	statistics

(1) _____ show that the number of U.S. museums is more than

15,000. The (2) _____ of one museum is Arab Americans.

Arab Americans have made (3) _____ contributions to

science. One woman (4) _____ politics for 57 years. Another

Arab American's ideas were (5) _____ by a U.S. president.

C **Write the word from the box that replaces the underlined words.**

modified	monitored	priority	radical	statistics

_____ 1. Thomas <u>observed</u> White House news for many years.

_____ 2. Kennedy <u>changed</u> a writer's idea to use in a speech.

_____ 3. <u>Numbers that have been counted</u> tell us that there are many U.S. museums.

_____ 4. Arab Americans are the <u>most important topic</u> for this museum.

_____ 5. A geologist proved a <u>very different</u> theory about Earth's continents.

Word Study   Multiple Meanings

A word often has more than one meaning. Read about two different meanings of *monitor.*

1 *monitor:*   (verb) to keep watch over something or someone; to observe critically

- monitor a game
- monitor behavior

- monitor what you eat
- monitor a science experiment

Parents **monitor** their children's behavior on the playground.

I **monitor** my growth by checking it every year.

2 *monitor:*   (noun) someone who supervises or watches over something or someone

- a hall monitor
- an election monitor

- a test monitor
- a safety monitor

The hall **monitor** tells students to walk, not run.

The election **monitor** counts votes for the town mayor.

Word Study Check Multiple Meanings

A For each numbered item, choose *a* or *b* as the correct meaning of the word in bold.

monitor
a. (verb) to keep watch over something or someone; to observe critically
b. (noun) someone who supervises or watches over something

1. _____ The class **monitor** returns homework to students.

2. _____ The referee **monitored** the soccer game.

3. _____ The nurse will **monitor** what patients eat.

4. _____ The election **monitor** helps citizens to vote.

B Write "Yes" or "No" to answer each question.

_____ 1. Can you monitor the weather?

_____ 2. Do doctors monitor their patients' health?

_____ 3. When you comb your hair, are you monitoring it?

_____ 4. Juan helps count votes. Is he an election monitor?

_____ 5. Elena took a test. Was she the test monitor?

_____ 6. Can you monitor attendance?

C Follow the directions below. Write your answers on the lines.

1. List two things you can **monitor**.

   _____

   _____

2. List two kinds of **monitors**.

   _____

   _____

Lesson 19 Wrap-up

 Talk About It

Discuss questions 1–5 with a partner.

Topic:
How I measure success

Details:

1. What goal is a high priority in your life?

2. How do you monitor your progress toward reaching that goal?

3. How can you use statistics to show if you are reaching it?

4. How might a radical change help you reach your goal?

5. How would you modify your behavior to reach your goal?

 Write About It

Write about measuring success on the lines below. Use ideas from Talk About It.

Topic:
I measure success by _____
_____.

Details:

1. One goal that is a high priority in my life is _____
_____.

2. I monitor my progress toward that goal by _____
_____.

3. I can use statistics to help show my progress by _____
_____.

4. A radical change might help me reach my goal by
_____
_____.

5. I would modify my behavior by _____
_____ to reach my goal.

Vocabulary in Context

Look at the photos and read the text. Respond to the text.

Many teens start their own businesses. Some teens mow lawns for a fee. Others make and sell jewelry.

One thing that encourages teens to start businesses is money. Another **incentive** for starting a business might be wanting to set and accomplish a personal goal. What are some other possible incentives?

Teens with a mowing business can create business cards listing mowing as their service. If they start planting and weeding too, they can **modify** the cards to includes these services.

A teen who makes jewelry might **refine** the style of her jewelry as she learns new skills. She could then modify her business card to parallel the change in the style of her jewelry.

Teens who run a business often make the business a **priority**. These young people choose to devote their time to the business instead of sports or clubs.

All business owners should have a **policy** of saving some of the money they earn for the future. How do large businesses apply the same principle?

Definitions

Read the definitions and example sentences.

incentive (in-sen′-tiv)

noun something that encourages an action or way of acting

The free candy was an **incentive** for new members to join the club.

modify (mä′-də-fī′)

verb to change or alter in some way

I **modify** my clothes to fit my personal style.

policy (pä′-lə-sē)

noun a set of rules or principles

The school's **policy** is to recycle all plastic bottles.

priority (prī-ôr′-ə-tē)

noun something that ranks high in importance

Linda's **priority** was finding her lost glasses.

refine (ri-fīn′)

verb to improve by removing imperfections

I **refined** my sketch by erasing and redrawing the nose.

Choose one word to draw in this space.

Definitions Check

A   Match the beginning of each sentence with its ending.

_____ 1. One incentive for studying   **a.** a recipe to make it less spicy.

_____ 2. A cook might modify   **b.** by fixing grammar mistakes.

_____ 3. The club's policy is that   **c.** is the chance to go to college.

_____ 4. A priority for comedy actors   **d.** members must wear their pins.

_____ 5. You can refine an essay   **e.** is entertaining an audience.

B   Put a check by the sentence that uses the bold word correctly.

_____ 1. Wanting a trophy is one **incentive** for entering a race.

_____   I left my **incentive** on the bench while I stretched.

_____ 2. Ana will **modify** the song by listening to it many times.

_____   Ana will **modify** the song by writing new words for it.

_____ 3. Most students know the school's attendance **policy.**

_____   The **policy** arrested the thief for stealing.

_____ 4. On the weekend, her **priority** is playing soccer with friends.

_____   She discussed the **priority** of the movie with her friends.

_____ 5. It is my job to **refine** and dry the plates after dinner.

_____   Mrs. Taft sent Lucy to a school to **refine** her manners.

C   Circle the answer to each question. The answer is in the question. The first one has been done for you.

1. Is a (prize) or a language an example of an _incentive_?

2. If you _modify_ a plan, do you change it or carry it out?

3. If you follow a _policy,_ do you follow a recipe or a rule?

4. Is a _priority_ something that is loud or important?

5. If you _refine_ something, do you make it better or worse?

Students participate in a business contest.

Business Success for Students

How can teens start businesses in their schools? Students from Santa Monica High School in California transformed the teachers' lounge into a café. They **modified** the menu of food that the school usually offered by featuring a salad bar and other healthful foods. They **refined** the room to make it look more like a café than a teachers' lounge. How do you think teachers responded to the new room?

These students had an extra **incentive** to launch their business. They qualified to enter a contest sponsored by the Students for the Advancement of Global Entrepreneurship (SAGE). This group's **policy** is motivate students to create businesses by sponsoring a contest. This contest became a **priority** for the students. They worked on their café business for one year. Then they traveled to New York, where their business competed against nine other student-run U.S. businesses.

Their café business was a hit! Judges awarded the Santa Monica students first place. This victory qualified them to enter the SAGE international contest. The students traveled to China to compete against student groups from ten countries. Once again, the California students took the top prize.

How do you think the judges measured the students' success?

Comprehension Check

A   **Write T if the sentence is true. Write F if the sentence is false.**

_____ 1. The students **modifed** the contest rules.

_____ 2. The café business was a **priority** for the students.

_____ 3. The students had the **incentive** of being in a movie.

_____ 4. Students **refined** the teachers' lounge to make it like a café.

_____ 5. The SAGE **policy** is to provide business incentives for students.

B   **Write the word from the box that completes each sentence.**

incentive	modify	policy	priority	refined

Students (1) _____ the teachers' lounge to make

a café. They had to (2) _____ the school's normal

food menu. Their (3) _____ for creating the café was

SAGE's business contest. One (4) _____ of SAGE

was to help students learn to run businesses by sponsoring a contest. For

the students, the contest was a (5) _____.

C   **Write the word from the box that replaces the underlined words.**

incentive	modify	policies	priority	refined

_____ 1. A café lounge could <u>change</u> teachers' diets.

_____ 2. The students <u>improved</u> their business skills through the contest.

_____ 3. Helping students become entrepreneurs is a <u>top goal</u> of business education.

_____ 4. Making money is only one possible <u>reason</u> for starting a business.

_____ 5. Saving money is a good <u>practice</u>.

Word Study Collocations

A collocation is a phrase or group of words that people use a lot. There are two collocations that use the word *priority.* They have different meanings.

1 *high priority:* **something that ranks very high in importance**
- Knowing how to swim is a **high priority** for my family because we live near a lake.
- We took the fastest route because getting a good seat at the concert was a **high priority.**

Ana practices her violin because playing well is a **high priority.**

Leaving work on time is a **high priority** for both of us.

2 *low priority:* **something that ranks very low in importance**
- We walked slowly around the park, because getting exercise was a **low priority** for us.
- Shopping was a **low priority** for Tan, so he did not stop at the store.

Buying new things is a **low priority** for Alba compared to saving money.

Fabio's test is still two weeks away, so studying today is a **low priority** for him.

Word Study Check Collocations

A Rewrite each sentence on the line below it. Replace the underlined words with a collocation from the box.

high priority	low priority

1. We sing in a choir because music is a <u>very important activity</u> for us.

   _____

2. For some people, traveling is a <u>last choice</u>.

   _____

3. For Mijal, the costume party is a <u>choice that is not interesting</u>.

   _____

B Circle the word that does not belong with the others in its row. The first one is done for you.

1. a high priority:

   necessary   (silly)   significant   considerable

2. a low priority:

   unimportant   worthless   major   unnecessary

3. a high priority:

   required   funny   first   important

C Complete the sentences below.

1. A high priority for me is _____.

2. When I am on vacation, _____ is a low priority for me.

3. Exercise is a high priority for some people because _____

   _____.

4. A high priority for my friends is _____.

5. A low priority for my friends is _____.

Lesson 20 Wrap-up

 Talk About It

Discuss questions 1–5 with a partner.

Topic:
Starting a business

Details:

1. What **incentive** might you have to start your own business?

2. What would be a **priority** of your business?

3. What is one **policy** your business would follow?

4. How would you need to **modify** your life to make time for a business?

5. How could you **refine** your plan for starting a business?

Write About It

Write about starting a business on the lines below. Use ideas from Talk About It.

Topic:
A business I would like to start is _____

_____.

Details:

1. My incentive for starting a business might be _____

_____.

2. A priority of my business would be _____

_____.

3. One policy my business would follow is _____

_____.

4. To make time for a business, I would modify _____

_____.

5. I might refine my business plan by _____

_____.

Vocabulary in Context

Look at the photos and read the text. Respond to the text.

Many teens have jobs. Making money is a powerful **incentive** to get and keep a job, but some people say teens should work for other reasons too. These people **advocate** teen employment because they say it teaches life skills.

What could a job teach you?

When you work day after day, you **refine** your skills. For example, you may make mistakes using a cash register at first, but eventually you'll become an expert.

What skills would you like to learn at a job?

If you work in restaurant, one part of your job is knowing the menu. Another **component** of your job is treating customers well. Workers should pay close attention to how they treat people. When you **monitor** your own behavior, you learn a valuable life skill.

Why is it important to know how to treat people?

Definitions

Read the definitions and example sentences.

advocate (ad'-və-kāt')

verb to speak or write in support of

The senators **advocate** spending more money on education.

component (kəm-pō'-nənt)

noun one of the parts that make up a whole

A keyboard is one **component** of a computer system.

incentive (in-sen'-tiv)

noun something that encourages an action or way of acting

My father gave me baseball tickets as an **incentive** to mow the lawn.

monitor (mä'-nə-tər)

verb to keep watch over something or someone

The doctor will **monitor** her patient throughout the day.

refine (ri-fīn')

verb to improve by removing imperfections

Vinh will **refine** his paper by correcting spelling mistakes.

Choose one word to draw in this space.

Definitions Check

A **Put a check by the answer to each question.**

1. Which sentence describes something that is a component?
   _____ The old car could not go fast.
   _____ A steering wheel is a part of a car.

2. Which sentence includes an example of an incentive?
   _____ Mina worked hard so she could win the trophy.
   _____ Leann's brother watches TV every night.

3. Which sentence describes someone who advocated something?
   _____ She spoke in favor of the proposed project.
   _____ The king left the country in the middle of the night.

4. Which sentence is an example of how someone can monitor something?
   _____ Chen checks his heart rate before and after he runs.
   _____ Paula left her dog at home when she went out.

B **Write the word from the box that completes each sentence.**

advocate	component	incentive	monitor	refine

1. I will _____ the recipe by using less flour.

2. The party was over, so I had no _____ to stay.

3. They _____ using the new plan.

4. Exercise is one _____ of a healthy lifestyle.

5. The coach will _____ my progress.

C **Complete the sentences below.**

1. One component of learning is _____.

2. One incentive to exercise is _____.

3. I often monitor _____.

4. Many people advocate _____.

5. I plan to refine _____.

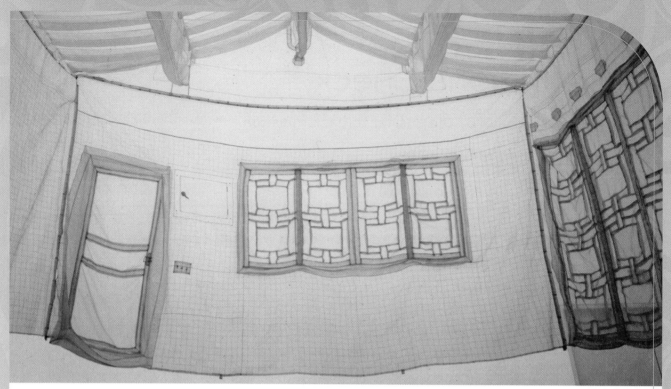

Do-Ho Suh created the artwork *Seoul Home/L.A. Home.*

A Successful Artist at Work

Artists have different reasons for creating art. Do-Ho Suh, a well-known Korean artist, had a strong **incentive** to create his artwork *Seoul Home/L.A. Home.* Suh lives in Los Angeles, but he grew up in Korea. He wanted to create a piece of art that would recreate his home in Korea. How would you recreate your home?

Suh first studied art in Korean schools, where teachers carefully **monitor** their students' work. Later he attended art schools in the United States, where teachers **advocate** a different approach. These teachers encouraged Suh to make art that expressed his feelings. One of his strongest feelings was how much he missed Korea.

Suh had the idea to bring his Korean home to the United States. This idea seemed impossible! Suh took time to **refine** his idea. He finally created *Seoul Home/L.A. Home*, a piece of art resembling a large tent, which recreates the look and feeling of his Korean home. One **component** of the tent is a green ceiling, like the ceiling of his Korean home.

For Do-Ho Suh, success meant finding a way to express his feelings. What does success mean to you?

Comprehension Check

A Write T if the sentence is true. Write F if the sentence is false.

_____ 1. A red ceiling is one **component** of *Seoul Home/L.A. Home.*

_____ 2. Do-Ho Suh's main **incentive** was to make money.

_____ 3. Suh **refined** the idea for *Seoul Home/L.A. Home* over time.

_____ 4. Both schools Suh attended **advocated** the same approach to art.

_____ 5. Suh's teachers in Korea carefully **monitored** his style.

B Write the word from the box that completes each sentence.

advocate	components	incentive	monitor	refine

Art schools (1) _____ different approaches to art.

Some teachers (2) _____ their students closely. But

all schools ask students to (3) _____ their work. For

Do-Ho Suh, recreating his Korean home in the United States was an

(4) _____ for creating art. His finished product was

made up of many (5) _____.

C Write the word from the box that replaces the underlined words.

advocate	component	incentive	monitor	refine

_____ 1. Money is not the only <u>reason</u> for creating art.

_____ 2. Some artists <u>speak in favor of</u> studying art in school.

_____ 3. Artists work hard to <u>remove imperfections from</u> their art.

_____ 4. Teachers may <u>watch over</u> art students' progress.

_____ 5. Color may be one <u>part</u> of a work of art.

Word Study The Root *voc*

The root of a word is the part that tells us the basic meaning of the word. The root *voc* comes from the Latin word *vox*, which means "voice." Some words that are built from this root are *advocate*, *vocation*, and *vocal*.

Word	Root	Meaning
advocate		to speak or write in support of
vocation	*voc* = voice	a career one feels called to do
vocal		belonging to or related to the voice

1 vocation (*voc* + *ation*)

The suffix *-ation* signifies "action."
Vocation is a noun that means "a career" or "a job one feels called to do."

My father works as a carpenter. That is his <u>job</u>.

I feel called to care for animals, so I will make it my <u>career</u>.

My father works as a carpenter. That is his **vocation**.

I feel called to care for animals, so I will make it my **vocation**.

2 vocal (*voc* + *al*)

The suffix *-al* signifies "belonging to" or "related to."
Vocal is an adjective that means "belonging to or related to the voice."

The tongue is a <u>voice-related</u> organ.

Lia enjoys giving performances <u>using her voice</u>.

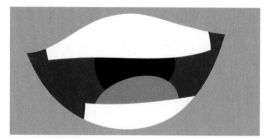

The tongue is a **vocal** organ.

Lia enjoys giving **vocal** performances.

Word Study Check The Root *voc*

A For each word, circle the root.

Example: e(voc)ative

1. advocate

2. vocation

3. vocal

B Circle the word that completes each sentence.

My chosen (**vocation, advocate**) is in musical performance. I am a
(**vocation, vocal**) performer and a guitarist. I (**vocal, advocate**) practicing a
lot and taking good care of your voice.

C Complete each sentence.

1. My future vocation will be in _____

_____.

2. A vocal performance I have heard is _____

_____.

3. I advocate _____

_____.

D Circle the word that has a very different meaning from the other three
words in its row.

1. favor   support   reject   advocate

2. mouth   local   voice   vocal

3. habit   vocation   job   work

Lesson 21 Wrap-up

 Talk About It

Discuss questions 1–5 with a partner.

Topic:
My idea of success

Details:

1. What is one important **component** of success?

2. What type of success do you **advocate**?

3. After you set goals for success, how can you **refine** them?

4. What **incentives** do you have to succeed?

5. How can you **monitor** your success?

 Write About It

Write about success on the lines below. Use ideas from Talk About It.

Topic:
My idea of success is _____

_____.

Details:

1. One important component of success is _____

_____.

2. The type of success I advocate is _____

_____.

3. I can refine my goals by _____

_____.

4. The incentives I have to succeed include _____

_____.

5. I can monitor my success by _____

_____.

Unit 7 Wrap-up

 Think About It

Think about the words you learned in Unit 7. Have you mastered them? Write each word under the right heading: Words I Have Mastered or Words I Need to Review. Make sentences using the words to prepare for the Unit Assessment.

Vocabulary Words

advocate	policy
component	priority
incentive	radical
modify	refine
monitor	statistics

Words I Have Mastered

_____   _____

_____   _____

_____   _____

_____   _____

Words I Need to Review

_____   _____

_____   _____

_____   _____

Practice Sentences

_____

_____

_____

_____

_____

_____

_____

Unit 7 Assessment

A Read the letters between Chinazor and Mrs. Sanabria, the owner of a gift shop.

Circle the word that completes each sentence.

Dear Mrs. Sanabria,

I would like to apply for a job in your gift shop. I love the gifts in your shop. Some of the designs are traditional and some are (**policy, radical**). They're all beautiful! An added (**incentive, policy**) for me is the chance to learn about your business.

My (**priority, component**) is to work in a place that uses my best skills. I can help you to (**modify, priority**) the gift displays. I can also (**radical, refine**) your system for recording sales data.

Sincerely,
Chinazor

Write a word from the box to complete each sentence.

advocate	component	monitor	policy	statistics

Dear Chinazor:

My (1) _____ is to help young people. That's why I

(2) _____ hiring teens for after-school jobs. Your letter

comes at a good time. I need a helper in the storeroom. An organized storeroom

is an important (3) _____ of my business. Your job would

be to keep (4) _____ about the merchandise on a

computer. You would (5) _____ the gifts in stock and

order more when necessary. Can you come to the shop on Wednesday?

Sincerely,
Alana Sanabria, Owner
Alana's Gift Shop

B Circle the letter of the answer that best completes each sentence.

1. Studying is a _____ for devoted students.
   a. last priority
   b. low priority
   c. high priority

2. Harold chose jewelry-making as his _____.
   a. advocate
   b. vocal
   c. vocation

3. The lifeguard _____ the swimmers.
   a. monitors
   b. modifies
   c. advocates

4. This group _____ protecting the environment.
   a. advocates
   b. vocal
   c. vocation

C Circle the letter of the answer that means the same thing as the underlined word or phrase.

1. The recess monitor told the children to come in.
   a. supervisor
   b. critic
   c. teacher

2. Her college major is vocal music.
   a. violin music
   b. folk music
   c. sung music

3. For Jerome, reading about sports is a low priority.
   a. something that is not fun
   b. something that is not urgent
   c. something that is not easy

4. I monitor my heart rate when I go running.
   a. test
   b. modify
   c. keep track of

D For each item, write a sentence that uses both words.

1. policy, statistics

   _____

   _____

2. component, priority

   _____

   _____

3. advocate, modify

   _____

   _____

What Makes a Great Story?

Vocabulary
acquire
available
circumstance
distinct
enforce
maintain
previous
resource
specific
transfer

Word Study
- Word Forms
- The Root *spec*
- Collocations

"The best stories are the ones I see around me every day. I see winning and losing. I see love and sadness. You have to pay attention to learn the endings."

Srdan is from Croatia.

Vocabulary in Context

Look at the photos and read the text. Respond to the text.

Storytelling is an ancient art. Some families continue to pass on their favorite stories from one generation to the next. Does your family **maintain** this kind of tradition?

Everyone has different experiences and a **distinct** way of seeing the world. When people share stories, they begin to understand each other better.

Many situations and events inspire people to tell stories. Think of a **circumstance** that you can tell a story about.

You can tell a story in a group by playing a game with your friends. To play One Word Story, you have to **enforce** the following rule: everyone takes turns contributing just one word at a time.

To learn storytelling from the experts, check out a storytelling video from your library. You will get an idea of the language and gestures that storytellers use. You can **acquire** some of their skills just by watching and listening to them.

What makes someone an entertaining storyteller?

Definitions

Read the definitions and example sentences.

acquire (ə-kwīr′)

verb to get as your own

The boys like to **acquire** toys from their older brother.

circumstance (sər′-kəm-stants)

noun a condition, situation, or event

The rain at the picnic was an unpleasant **circumstance.**

distinct (di-stinkt′)

adjective different in quality or kind

Clara and Dolores dress in **distinct** ways.

enforce (en-fôrs′)

verb to cause people to obey

Police officers **enforce** traffic laws.

maintain (mān-tān′)

verb to keep something as it is

Marisol exercises often to **maintain** her health.

Choose one word to draw in this space.

200

Definitions Check

A
Write the word from the box that matches the two examples in each item.

| acquire | circumstance | distinct | enforce | maintain |

1. _____
two different languages
an apple and a carrot

2. _____
to receive a book as a present
to learn a new skill

3. _____
to make people follow rules
to arrest someone for breaking a law

4. _____
to keep a friendship for many years
to remain healthy

B
Write the word from the box that relates to each group of words.

| acquire | circumstance | distinct | enforce | maintain |

_____ **1.** different, separate, unique

_____ **2.** sustain, keep, continue

_____ **3.** force, require, demand

_____ **4.** get, gain, obtain

_____ **5.** event, situation, condition

C
Write the word from the box that answers each question.

| acquire | circumstance | distinct | enforce | maintain |

1. Which word goes with *to keep your room clean*? _____

2. Which word goes with *to make someone pay a fine*? _____

3. Which word goes with *an unusual pattern*? _____

4. Which word goes with *an event*? _____

5. Which word goes with *to buy something*? _____

A storyteller performs at the festival.

The National Storytelling Festival

Every year the town of Jonesborough, Tennessee, hosts the National Storytelling Festival. Professional storytellers tell stories for three days! They come from around the world, and storytelling fans **acquire** their tickets months ahead of time.

A high school teacher came up with the idea of holding the festival. The **circumstance** that gave him the idea was a moment with his students. While listening to the radio, they heard someone telling a great story. The students said they would like to listen to good stories in person. A few years later, the teacher organized the first National Storytelling Festival.

The festival brings together a diverse group of professional storytellers. Each storyteller has a **distinct** style. A storyteller may incorporate singing, dancing, or musical instruments. The festival officials **enforce** a one-hour time limit on each show, but they allow the storytellers to decide how to present their stories.

The National Storytelling Festival has caused new interest in storytelling. The festival has helped to **maintain** enthusiasm for this traditional art form. The people who go to the festival believe that storytelling is important because it brings people together.

Do you think storytelling is important? Why or why not?

Comprehension Check

A Write T if the sentence is true. Write F if the sentence is false.

_____ 1. Festival officials **enforce** a time limit on each performance.

_____ 2. Storytellers **acquire** musical instruments at the festival.

_____ 3. The festival helps **maintain** an interest in storytelling.

_____ 4. The storytellers at the festival have **distinct** styles.

_____ 5. The **circumstance** that led to the establishment of the festival is unknown.

B Write the word from the box that completes each sentence.

acquire	circumstance	distinct	enforce	maintain

A high school teacher heard an entertaining story on the radio. This

(1) _____ inspired him to start a storytelling festival.

The festival helps (2) _____ an interest in storytelling.

Fans (3) _____ tickets months in advance. The

festival invites storytellers with (4) _____ styles.

Officials (5) _____ a time limit on each show.

C Write the word from the box that replaces the underlined words.

acquire	circumstances	distinct	enforce	maintain

_____ 1. People often <u>get</u> tickets to the festival early.

_____ 2. The <u>situations and events</u> described in each story are unique.

_____ 3. Professional storytellers help <u>to keep alive</u> the art of storytelling.

_____ 4. Officials <u>make people obey</u> rules at the festival.

_____ 5. This festival is <u>different</u> from other festivals.

Word Study Word Forms

Words often have several different forms. Read below about some of the different word forms of *distinct*.

1 *distinction* (noun)

A *distinction* is a difference.

A skateboard is clearly **distinct** from a scooter.

There is a clear **distinction** between a skateboard and a scooter.

We recognize that a circle and a square are **distinct** shapes.

We recognize the **distinction** between a circle and a square.

2 *distinctive* (adjective)

If something is *distinctive,* it is clearly different or special.

Venus flytraps are **distinct** from other plants.

Venus flytraps are **distinctive** plants.

Peacocks have feathers that are **distinct** from the feathers of other birds.

Peacocks have **distinctive** feathers.

Word Study Check Word Forms

A Circle the word that completes each sentence.

Horses and zebras are two (**distinct, distinction**) animals. The (**distinctive, distinction**) between the animals is easy to see. Zebras have a (**distinct, distinctive**) striped pattern.

B Complete each sentence.

1. Two distinct types of music are _____

_____.

2. The biggest distinction between last year and this year is _____

_____.

3. Referees wear distinctive uniforms because _____

_____.

C Match each word to its meaning.

_____ **1.** distinct   **a.** clearly different or special

_____ **2.** distinction   **b.** difference

_____ **3.** distinctive   **c.** different in quality or kind

D Write the word from the box that completes each sentence.

distinct	distinction	distinctive

1. They saw a clear _____ between the two paintings.

2. A poem is _____ from a short story.

3. The owner gave her store a _____ name.

Lesson 22 Wrap-up

Talk About It

Discuss questions 1–5 with a partner.

Topic:
How to tell a good story

Details:

1. What kind of **circumstance** makes a good story?

2. What is a story you have told that is **distinct** from ordinary stories?

3. How did you make sure your audience **maintained** interest in your story?

4. What rules should a storyteller **enforce** while telling a story?

5. How could you **acquire** the skills to become a better storyteller?

Write About It

Write about storytelling on the lines below. Use ideas from Talk About It.

Topic:
To tell a good story, you have to _____

_____ .

Details:

1. One kind of circumstance that makes a good story is _____

_____ .

2. A story I have told that was distinct is _____

_____ .

3. I made sure that my audience maintained interest in

my story by _____ .

4. When I tell a story, I enforce a rule that _____

_____ .

5. I could acquire the skills to become a better storyteller by

_____ .

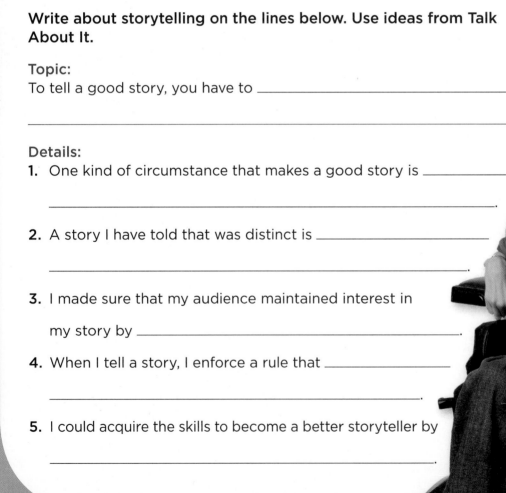

Vocabulary in Context

Look at the photos and read the text. Respond to the text.

A great story can make readers laugh, cry, or even feel terrified! To communicate a great story, it helps if you show your emotions. You can show emotions in writing as well as speech. Use descriptive words, and don't simply tell the general parts of the story. Add **specific** details.

What stories do you have in your mind? Can you **transfer** them to paper?

There are many tools you can use to help you write stories. Computers at a library may be **available** to you. Books in the library can help you choose words. Try to use words that add color to your writing, such as *dazzling* instead of *bright*. Gradually you will **acquire** a large vocabulary.

Great stories are often based on universal themes. Love, courage, and struggle are examples of universal themes. Some writers try to develop these themes in traditional ways. Others try to present these and other themes differently, from a **distinct** point of view. What theme would you like to write about?

Definitions

Read the definitions and example sentences.

acquire (ə-kwīr′)

verb to get as your own

Hector helped me to **acquire** new skateboard skills.

available (ə-vā′-lə-bəl)

adjective ready or able to be used

Only a few tickets are **available** for the concert.

distinct (di-stinkt′)

adjective different in quality or kind

Each member of the school choir has a **distinct** voice.

specific (spi-si′-fik)

adjective definite; particular

Nadia wanted a **specific** type of rock for her collection.

transfer (trans′-fər)

verb to move from one person or one place to another

Ivette had to **transfer** to a new school this year.

Choose one word to draw in this space.

208

Definitions Check

A **Match the beginning of each sentence with its ending.**

_____ 1. Big companies often acquire   **a.** type of butterfly.

_____ 2. The only food available   **b.** smaller companies.

_____ 3. The distinct bands of color   **c.** is the rice on the table.

_____ 4. A monarch is a specific   **d.** made the fish easy to see.

_____ 5. Help transfer the suitcases   **e.** from the van to the house.

B **Put a check by the sentence that uses the bold word correctly.**

_____ 1. He needs a **specific** kind of apple to make this dessert.

_____   She has **specific** hands because she can play the piano.

_____ 2. Tan loves to walk among the **available** trees in the forest.

_____   The pencils in the drawer are **available** for everyone to use.

_____ 3. Nina will **transfer** the file from her computer to Bob's.

_____   Pablo and Luisa know how to **transfer** on the dance floor.

_____ 4. When I go to Haiti, I will **acquire** members of my family.

_____   I **acquire** knowledge of my past as I listen to family stories.

_____ 5. I can identify the lead singer because her voice is **distinct**.

_____   You must be **distinct** to ask people about their feelings.

C **Circle the answer to each question. The answer is in the question. The first one has been done for you.**

1. If an item is *available,* can you (buy it) or do you have to wait?

2. When you *transfer* something, do you move it or leave it alone?

3. If a house is *distinct* from others, is it similar or different?

4. If you give a *specific* example, is it general or detailed?

5. Which can you *acquire,* a new suit or a daydream?

Christopher Paolini writes in Montana, U.S.A.

Teen Author Writes a Great Story

Who do you think can beat J. K. Rowling, the author of the Harry Potter books, on a best-seller list? Meet Christopher Paolini, a young man who started writing as a teenager. Paolini offers a **distinct** style of fantasy literature. His first two books, *Eragon* and *Eldest,* have made best-seller lists. Readers waited for the third book to become **available.**

Paolini began writing his first novel, *Eragon,* when he was fifteen years old. In this book, Paolini's general interest in dragons became a very **specific** dragon named Saphira that lives in a magical forest. Paolini discovered that it was easy for him to **transfer** his ideas from his head to paper. Paolini's parents edited his writing before a publisher bought the rights to the books. At first Paolini did not want to accept suggestions about ways to change his stories. But once he began working with the publisher, Paolini learned how other people's ideas could help.

Paolini believes that writers should **acquire** the habit of writing daily. He knows from experience that persistence leads to success. He also believes that writers should choose topics that fascinate them. Dragons were the topic that fascinated him. What is your topic?

Comprehension Check

A **Write T if the sentence is true. Write F if the sentence is false.**

_____ 1. Christopher Paolini uses a **distinct** style in his stories.

_____ 2. Readers waited for Paolini's third book to become **available.**

_____ 3. It was a challenge for Paolini to **transfer** his ideas to paper.

_____ 4. Paolini could not think of anything **specific** to write.

_____ 5. Paolini says writers should **acquire** the habit of writing daily.

B **Write the word from the box that completes each sentence.**

acquire	available	distinct	specific	transfer

Christopher Paolini has a (1) _____ writing style. Many

readers anxiously waited for his books to become (2) _____.

His books are about a (3) _____ dragon named Saphira. It

is easy for Paolini to (4) _____ his ideas to paper. Paolini

believes that writers should (5) _____ good habits.

C **Write the word from the box that replaces the underlined words.**

acquired	available	distinct	specific	transfer

_____ 1. Paolini is <u>willing</u> to talk to the public.

_____ 2. Because most teens don't write novels, Christopher Paolini's life is <u>different from theirs</u>.

_____ 3. Paolini is interested in dragons in general, but he writes about a <u>particular</u> dragon named Saphira.

_____ 4. Writers <u>move</u> their ideas from their minds to paper.

_____ 5. Many fans have <u>gotten</u> their own copies of Paolini's books.

Word Study   The Suffix *-able*

A suffix is a part of a word that has a meaning of its own. It comes at the end of a word. A common suffix is *-able*. Some words that have this suffix are *available*, *enjoyable*, *attainable*, and *adjustable*.

Word	Root	Suffix	Meaning
enjoyable	*enjoy* = to be happy with		able to be enjoyed
attainable	*attain* = to reach or achieve through effort	*-able* = able to be, that can be	able to be attained
adjustable	*adjust* = to adjust		able to be adjusted

1   *enjoyable* (*enjoy* + *able*)

The root *enjoy* means "to be happy with" or "to take pleasure in."
Enjoyable is an adjective that means "able to be enjoyed."

Finger painting is an activity children are <u>able to enjoy</u>.

Finger painting is an **enjoyable** activity for children.

Walking on the beach is a form of exercise <u>people are able to enjoy</u>.

Walking on the beach is an **enjoyable** form of exercise.

2   *adjustable* (*adjust* + *able*)

The root *adjust* means "to adapt" or "to get used to."
Adjustable is an adjective that means "able to be adjusted."

The height of the keyboard is a feature that is <u>able to be adjusted</u>.

The height of the keyboard is an **adjustable** feature.

The back of the dentist's chair is <u>able to be adjusted</u>.

The back of the dentist's chair is **adjustable**.

Word Study Check The Suffix *-able*

 A For each word, circle the suffix and underline the root.

Example: <u>avail</u>(able)

1. enjoyable

2. adjustable

3. attainable

B Circle the word that completes each sentence.

Some people find that building their own furniture is (**adjustable, enjoyable**). They can use tools and supplies that are (**available, enjoyable**) at many stores. People who build children's furniture might make chairs that are (**adjustable, available**) for different heights.

C Complete each sentence.

1. I often find books available in _____

_____.

2. For me an enjoyable activity is _____

_____.

3. Something adjustable that is useful is _____

_____.

D Circle the word that has a very different meaning from the other three words in its row.

1. available   hidden   present   ready

2. enjoyable   happy   fun   difficult

3. adjustable   moveable   solid   changeable

Lesson 23 Wrap-up

 Talk About It

Discuss questions 1–5 with a partner.

Topic:
How I could write a book

Details:

1. Where could you **acquire** ideas for a book?

2. What tools are **available** to help you write a book?

3. How could you make your writing style **distinct**?

4. What **specific** subjects would you like to write about?

5. What ideas do you want to **transfer** to your book?

 Write About It

Write about writing a book on the lines below. Use ideas from Talk About It.

Topic:
I think that writing a book would be _____
_____.

Details:

1. I could acquire ideas for a book from _____
_____.

2. Some tools that are available to help me write a book are
_____.

3. I could make my writing style distinct by _____
_____.

4. Some specific subjects I like to write about are
_____.

5. Some ideas I would like to transfer to paper are
_____
_____.

214

Vocabulary in Context

Look at the photos and read the text. Respond to the text.

A picture can be a photograph, a drawing, or a painting. Of the three kinds of pictures, a photograph is usually the most exact. For example, a photo of an earthquake can show exactly where the damage is. It can also show the the reaction of a **specific** person.

How does the photo show how an earthquake affected this person?

A drawing can contain information just like a photo. Ancient drawings can be a **resource** for people who study the past. They can show how people from **previous** cultures lived. Many of these drawings are found on pottery.

What other stories can a drawing tell?

Paintings tell stories too. Many paintings are **available** for the public to see. People in many cities can go to museums and enjoy looking at paintings from many time periods. Experts work to **maintain** the original beauty of artwork for future generations. They clean and protect the paintings.

What can you learn from paintings in a museum?

Definitions

Read the definitions and example sentences.

available (ə-vā′-lə-bəl)

adjective ready or able to be used

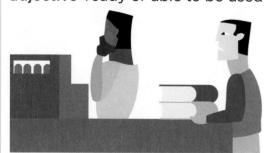

The salesperson was not **available** because he was on the phone.

maintain (mān-tān′)

verb to keep something as it is

Kee works hard to **maintain** the beauty of his yard.

previous (prē′-vē-əs)

adjective before, in time or order; earlier

Lola likes her job at the restaurant better than her **previous** job.

resource (rē′-sōrs′)

noun something that provides a supply to satisfy a need

Water is a scarce **resource** in some regions.

specific (spi-si′-fik)

adjective definite; particular

Mario is looking for a **specific** kind of shirt.

Choose one word to draw in this space.

216

Definitions Check

A   Put a check by the answer to each question.

1. Which sentence is an example of someone who is available?
   _____ I told my brother I can go with him to the soccer game.
   _____ I told my brother I would be busy during the soccer game.

2. Which sentence describes something that someone is maintaining?
   _____ Teodora cuts the grass every week.
   _____ Teodora looked out over the ocean.

3. Which sentence describes something that happened at a previous time?
   _____ I had a sandwich for lunch yesterday.
   _____ I will have soup for lunch today.

4. Which sentence is an example of someone who wants something specific?
   _____ Jamil will eat any kind of cereal that he can find.
   _____ Jamil will only eat his Crunchy Flakes brand cereal.

B   Write the word from the box that completes each sentence.

available	maintain	previous	resource	specific

1. This year was colder than the _____ one.

2. I am _____ for lunch at 12:30.

3. An encyclopedia is a good _____ for doing research.

4. I try to _____ a good attitude when I face a challenge.

5. Our coach taught us exercises to help _____ muscles.

C   Complete the sentences below.

1. It is important to me to maintain _____.

2. In previous school years I have _____.

3. One specific movie I like is _____.

4. One resource I use to find information is _____.

5. If I had more time available, I would _____.

This is part of a Mayan mural discovered in 2001.

A Mayan Mural Tells a Story

In 2001, archaeologists discovered a story that was almost 2,000 years old! It was a mural, or a painting on a wall. It was buried under a pyramid in the city of San Bartolo, Guatemala. The mural was painted by the Maya people of Central America. On **previous** trips, archaeologists had uncovered other murals. But the painting at San Bartolo is the oldest Mayan mural ever found.

Despite its age, the mural looks almost new. The layer of mud that had covered the mural actually helped to **maintain** it over the years. Because the art is easy to see, the mural is an important historical **resource**. It gives people new information about the ancient Maya civilization.

Each part of the mural shows a **specific** step in the creation story of the Maya. The first part shows how the god of maize, or corn, established the oceans, the land, and the sky. The second part shows the maize god planting a tree in the middle of the world and then making himself king. Another section shows a human king. Archaeologists took photographs of the mural and made them **available** to the public in 2005.

What is a benefit of learning about people who lived long ago?

Comprehension Check

A Write T if the sentence is true. Write F if the sentence is false.

_____ 1. Photographs of the mural were **available** 2,000 years ago.

_____ 2. Mud helped to **maintain** the mural over the years.

_____ 3. The mural is an important **resource** for archaeologists.

_____ 4. Each **specific** section of the mural tells the same story.

_____ 5. **Previous** studies uncovered murals that were 5,000 years old.

B Write the word from the box that completes each sentence.

available	maintain	previous	resource	specific

Pictures of the San Bartolo mural became (1) _____

to the public in 2005. Mud had helped to (2) _____

the painting over the years. Archeologists had found other murals in

(3) _____ studies. Experts think the painting is a

great (4) _____. Each (5) _____

section of the mural tells a different part of a creation story.

C Write the word from the box that replaces the underlined words.

available	maintain	previous	resource	specific

_____ 1. Mud helped to <u>keep up</u> the mural's condition.

_____ 2. The mural tells a <u>particular</u> story about the god of maize who makes himself king.

_____ 3. I hope that a book about the mural will be <u>ready</u> in bookstores soon.

_____ 4. The mural is a <u>source of knowledge</u> for historians.

_____ 5. In <u>earlier</u> studies, archaeologists found other murals.

Word Study   Collocations

A collocation is a phrase or group of words that people use a lot. There are two collocations that use the word *resources.* They have different meanings.

1 *natural resources:*   **materials and energy from nature**
- Water is one of our most important natural resources.
- Wind is another one of our natural resources.

Our national parks have many natural resources.

Diamonds and gold are natural resources.

2 *human resources:*   **people who use their skills to do work for a company or organization**
- A company's human resources are very important.
- The strongest part of our college is its human resources.

The interview was with Mrs. Baez, who manages the company's human resources.

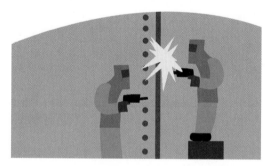

The human resources at a factory are key to the factory's success.

Word Study Check Collocations

A Rewrite each sentence on the line below it. Replace the underlined words with a collocation from the box.

human resources	natural resources

1. Companies need <u>skilled workers</u> to produce products.

   _____

2. Miners work to find <u>materials such as iron and zinc</u> in the earth.

   _____

3. We need to protect Earth's <u>water, air, and trees</u>.

   _____

B Circle the word that does not belong with the others in its row. The first one is done for you.

1. natural resources: forests   lakes   minerals   (buildings)

2. human resources: workers   employees   air   people

3. natural resources: water   computers   plants   coal

C Complete the sentences below.

1. If we do not use natural resources wisely, _____

   _____.

2. Without human resources, _____

   _____.

3. Natural resources are important because _____

   _____.

4. Human resources at a shopping mall might include _____

   _____.

5. Natural resources in my community include _____.

Lesson 24 Wrap-up

 **Talk About It**

Discuss questions 1–5 with a partner.

Topic:
A story from my life told through a book of pictures

Details:

1. What **available** tools will you use to create your book?

2. What is one **resource** that could help you tell your story?

3. What **specific** part of your life will your story be about?

4. What **previous** events will you concentrate on?

5. How will you **maintain** your readers' interest in the story?

✏️ Write About It

Write about a story from your life on the lines below. Use ideas from Talk About It.

Topic:
The story from my life that I want to tell is about _____

_____ .

Details:

1. I will create a book using tools available to me, including _____

_____ .

2. One resource that could help me tell my story is _____

_____ .

3. The specific part of my life that my story will be about is

_____ .

4. Previous events that I will tell about are _____

_____ .

5. I will maintain my readers' interest in the story by

_____

_____ .

Unit 8 Wrap-up

 ## Think About It

Think about the words you learned in Unit 8. Have you mastered them? Write each word under the right heading: Words I Have Mastered or Words I Need to Review. Make sentences using the words to prepare for the Unit Assessment.

Words I Have Mastered

_____   _____

_____   _____

_____   _____

_____   _____

Words I Need to Review

_____   _____

_____   _____

Practice Sentences

_____

_____

_____

_____

_____

_____

_____

_____

Unit 8 Assessment

A Read the entries in this travel journal.

Circle the word that completes each sentence.

July 9

Today I woke up with no (**specific, available**) plans. After breakfast I decided to visit the Argentinian modern art museum, which (**enforces, maintains**) a beautiful collection. The photography section recently (**acquired, transferred**) a new exhibit. I had no (**available, previous**) interest in photography, but I enjoyed this exhibit so much that I decided to buy a book about it. The book is an excellent (**circumstance, resource**). I can't wait to show it to my family and friends.

Write a word from the box to complete each sentence.

available	circumstance	distinct	enforces	transfer

July 10

I visited San Telmo, a neighborhood in Buenos Aires, because no tickets were (1) _____ for the soccer match I wanted to see. I had to (2) _____ from a bus to a train. Then it started to rain, a (3) _____ I had not planned for. Still, the trip was worth it! I think it's great that the government (4) _____ laws to protect old buildings. Now I have beautiful memories of this historic area that is (5) _____ from every other place I've seen.

B Circle the letter of the answer that best completes each sentence.

1. Estela thought the rock concert was _____.
   a. adjustable
   b. attainable
   c. enjoyable

2. Toucans are unique birds that have large, _____ beaks.
   a. distinction
   b. distinctive
   c. distinct

3. Forests and lakes are examples of _____ resources.
   a. previous
   b. natural
   c. human

4. The _____ hat is made to fit anyone's head.
   a. adjustable
   b. attainable
   c. enjoyable

C Circle the letter of the answer that means the same thing as the underlined word or phrase.

1. Mrs. Cha's job is to manage human resources.
   a. skilled workers
   b. computer technology
   c. natural chemicals

2. What is the distinction between a rat and a mouse?
   a. perspective
   b. circumstance
   c. difference

3. The bicycle seat is adjustable. I can make it higher or lower.
   a. able to be changed
   b. able to be achieved
   c. able to be liked

4. The landscape artist has a distinctive style.
   a. final
   b. similar
   c. special

D For each item, write a sentence that uses both words.

1. available, resource

   _____

   _____

2. acquire, specific

   _____

   _____

3. enforce, maintain

   _____

   _____

My Notes

My Notes

228

My Notes

230

Writing Checklist

1. I followed the directions for writing.
2. My writing shows that I read and understood the discussion questions.
3. I capitalized the names of people and the proper names of places and things.
4. I read aloud my writing and listened for missing words.
5. I used a dictionary to check words that didn't look right.

Use the chart below to check off the things on the list that you have done.

Lesson Numbers	✔ Writing Checklist Numbers					Lesson Numbers					
	1	2	3	4	5		1	2	3	4	5
1						13					
2						14					
3						15					
4						16					
5						17					
6						18					
7						19					
8						20					
9						21					
10						22					
11						23					
12						24					

Glossary

A

acquire (ə-kwīr′)   *v.* to get as your own   pp. 200, 208

advocate (ad′-və-kāt′)   *v.* to speak or write in support of   p. 188

alternative (ôl-tər′-nə-tiv)   *n.* a different option; a choice between two or more things   p. 96

apparently (ə-par′-ənt-lē)   *adv.* seemingly; according to what you can see   pp. 116, 124

appropriate (ə-prō′-prē-ət)   *adj.* fitting or suitable   p. 48

aspect (as′-pekt′)   *n.* a particular part, feature, or characteristic of something   pp. 32, 48

assess (ə-ses′)   *v.* to evaluate; to determine the significance of something   pp. 124, 132

attain (ə-tān′)   *v.* to reach or arrive at; to accomplish   p. 104

attitude (a′-tə-tüd′)   *n.* a mental state or feeling   p. 20

attribute (ə-tri′-būt′)   *v.* to think of as caused by   pp. 152, 160

available (ə-vā′-lə-bəl)   *adj.* ready or able to be used   pp. 208, 216

C

circumstance (sər′-kəm-stants)   *n.* a condition, situation, or event   p. 200

colleague (kä′-lēg)   *n.* someone who works in the same place or at the same type of job   p. 68

compatible (kəm-pa′-tə-bəl)   *adj.* able to exist or function well with another   pp. 60, 76

compensate (käm′-pən-sāt′)   *v.* to make up for   p. 60

component (kəm-pō′-nənt)   *n.* one of the parts that make up a whole   p. 188

conceive (kən-sēv′)   *v.* to form or develop in the mind   p. 152

concentrate (kän′-sən-trāt′)   *v.* to focus or center your attention on something   pp. 88, 104

concept (kän′-sept′)   *n.* a general idea or thought   pp. 152, 160

considerable (kən-si′-dər-ə-bəl)   *adj.* significant; worthy of notice   pp. 144, 152

consist (kən-sist′)   *v.* to be formed or made up of   pp. 116, 124

contrast (kən-trast′)   *v.* to find differences between two or more people or things   p. 20

convert (kən-vərt′)   *v.* to change something into something else   p. 144

D

deviate (dē′-vē-āt′) *v.* to turn away from a course or path   p. 124

devoted (di-vō′-tid) *adj.* loyal; dedicated   pp. 4, 12

distinct (di-stinkt′) *adj.* different in quality or kind   pp. 200, 208

distribute (di-stri′-būt) *v.* to deliver or give out to several people or groups   p. 76

diverse (dī-vərs′) *adj.* made up of various qualities or kinds   pp. 32, 48

document (dä′-kyə-mənt′) *n.* something written or printed that gives information or proof   p. 132

E

element (e′-lə-mənt) *n.* a part of a whole   pp. 4, 12

enforce (en-fôrs′) *v.* to cause people to obey   p. 200

enhance (in-hans′) *v.* to make greater in beauty, quality, or value; to add to   pp. 40, 48

evaluate (i-val′-ū-āt′) *v.* to examine and judge carefully   p. 76

evolve (i-välv′) *v.* to develop over time or in stages   p. 32

exceed (ik-sēd′) *v.* to go beyond the limit of   pp. 60, 68

expand (ik-spand′) *v.* to make or grow larger   p. 48

external (ek-stər′-nəl) *adj.* on the outside   p. 88

F

flexible (flek′-sə-bəl) *adj.* easy to bend without breaking   p. 40

I

incentive (in-sen′-tiv) *n.* something that encourages an action or way of acting   pp. 180, 188

incorporate (in-kôr′-pə-rāt′) *v.* to combine a part or parts into a larger whole   p. 40

indicate (in′-də-kāt′) *v.* to point out or show   pp. 88, 96

inevitable (i-ne′-və-tə-bəl) *adj.* sure to happen   p. 144

intense (in-tens′) *adj.* extreme in strength or degree   p. 4

internal (in-tər′-nəl) *adj.* on the inside   pp. 88, 104

invest (in-vest′) *v.* to put money, time, or energy into something for later benefit   p. 116

M

maintain (mān-tān′) *v.* to keep something as it is   pp. 200, 216

maximize (mak′-sə-mīz) *v.* to increase as much as possible   pp. 144, 160

minimum (mi′-nə-məm) *adj.* smallest number; least amount necessary   p. 116

modify (mä′-də-fī′) *v.* to change or alter in some way   pp. 172, 180

monitor (mä′-nə-tər) *v.* to keep watch over something or someone pp. 172, 188

mutual (mū′-chōo-əl) *adj.* something shared between two or more people or things pp. 68, 76

O

objective (əb-jek′-tiv) *n.* a goal or an aim p. 96

overall (ō′-vər-ôl′) *adj.* including everyone or everything p. 4

P

persist (pər-sist′) *v.* to refuse to stop or give up; to remain in existence pp. 144, 152

philosophy (fə-lä′-sə-fē) *n.* a system of ideas and beliefs p. 160

policy (pä′-lə-sē) *n.* a set of rules or principles p. 180

positive (pä′-zə-tiv) *adj.* favorable; good pp. 12, 20

potential (pə-ten′-shəl) *n.* a skill or ability that can develop pp. 12, 20

practitioner (prak-ti′-shə-nər) *n.* a person who works in a trade, field, or profession p. 160

previous (prē′-vē-əs) *adj.* before, in time or order; earlier p. 216

principle (prin′-sə-pəl) *n.* a rule or belief that forms the basis for behavior or actions pp. 4, 20

priority (prī-ôr′-ə-tē) *n.* something that ranks high in importance pp. 172, 180

promote (prə-mōt′) *v.* to aid or support the progress of something pp. 96, 104

R

radical (ra′-di-kəl) *adj.* far from the usual; extreme p. 172

refine (ri-fīn′) *v.* to improve by removing imperfections pp. 180, 188

resource (rē′-sōrs′) *n.* something that provides a supply to satisfy a need p. 216

S

significant (sig-ni′-fi-kənt) *adj.* important; meaningful; noteworthy pp. 88, 96

specific (spi-si′-fik) *adj.* definite; particular pp. 208, 216

statistics (stə-tis′-tiks) *n.* information gathered in the form of numbers p. 172

status (sta′-təs) *n.* a person or thing's position in relation to others p. 68

strategy (stra′-tə-jē) *n.* a plan of action to accomplish a goal pp. 124, 132

substitute (səb′-stə-tōot′) *v.* to put in the place of someone or something else p. 104

sustain (sə-stān′)   *v.* to maintain or keep in existence   p. 12

T

transfer (trans′-fər)   *v.* to move from one person or place to another   p. 208

transform (trans-fôrm′)   *v.* to change in nature or condition   pp. 32, 40

transport (trans-pôrt′)   *v.* to carry from one place to another   pp. 60, 76

U

undertake (ən′-dər-tāk′)   *v.* to take responsibility for; to attempt   pp. 60, 68

unique (yoo-nēk′)   *adj.* being the only one of its type   pp. 32, 40

V

virtual (vər′-chə-wəl)   *adj.* not real; computer-generated   pp. 116, 132

W

welfare (wel′-fer′)   *n.* a state of well-being   p. 132

Image Credits